A New Criminal Type in Jakarta

A New Criminal Type in Jakarta

Counter-Revolution Today

James T. Siegel

Duke University Press

Durham and London 1998

© 1998 Duke University Press
All rights reserved Printed in the United States of America
on acid-free paper ∞
Typeset in Minion by Keystone Typesetting, Inc.
Library of Congress Cataloging-in-Publication Data appear
on the last printed page of this book.

For Anne Berger

Thus the revolution never became more than a "national revolution"; it ended in 1949. . . . Long after Indonesian sovereignty was recognized by the world, the search for 100 per cent merdeka [liberty] was to continue and was to remain sentenced to disappointment. But the hopes are still with us.—B.R. O'G. Anderson, 1972

Contents

Acknowledgments

I thank Ben Anderson and John Pemberton for commenting on parts of the manuscript, and I acknowledge Rudolf Mrazek for his comments and for his work on technology in colonial Indonesia, which promises to give us an entirely new picture of the period. Stimulated by the pressure of his thinking I was led to consider the role of the camera in Indonesia's New Order and, indeed, much else.

This book is for Anne Berger, the Annetonym of these terms of the title: "criminal," "counter-revolution," "Jakarta," "type."

A New Criminal Type in Jakarta

Introduction: Killing Those in One's Own Image

Indonesian National Violence

Most peoples of the world kill those they want to consider other than themselves: Hutus and Tutsis murder each other, as do Serbs and Croats, to take only recent examples. There is another type of massacre, however, in which one kills those in one's own image. The history of the Indonesian nation holds three clear examples. The Indonesian revolution began in 1945 and culminated in 1949 with the transfer of sovereignty from the Dutch to the independent state. In 1948 during the revolution nationalists fought communists, who were also nationalists, resulting in a number of dead that has never been estimated but which, it is agreed, was large. There was no doubt that both sides were comprised of "Indonesians." Then in 1965 came the massacre of Indonesian communists and those accused of being communists. This is clearly the largest in scale of the three, with many hundreds of thousands, perhaps more, murdered. In 1983 and 1984 came the events I will describe. At that time, "criminals," many of whom had until that point been employed by the government party, were killed by the thousands by the government.

There are other incidents of major violence in Indonesia: the revolution against the Dutch from 1946 to 1949 and the aggression against East Timor. In the first case one has to count not only Dutch deaths, but also the killings of Indonesians considered traitors either because they formed part of the Dutch armed forces or their civilian bureaucracy, or they were ordinary civilians thought to have betrayed the nation. No reliable figures are available. In the case of East Timor, a foreign territory was invaded and annexed and, as a direct or indirect result, it is estimated that a third of the population, over 200,000 people to date have died. But from our point of view, this case, like the revolution, is ambiguous; nonetheless it is clear that, as during the revolution when many were killed because they were Indonesians (traitors), the Indonesian government considers the East Timorese to be Indonesians and kills them on that assumption. One can add to these the aggression against Muslims in West Java and elsewhere.

One has to further add to this list; there has been violence against "Chinese" at various times in the nation's history. I put "Chinese" in quotes because aggression against them is inextricably bound up with the definition of their citizenship, with their loyalty to the nation, and their participation in the revolution. The insistence that they are not Indonesian, whether by citizenship or by sentiment, is, of course, always set against the possibility that they are members of the nation, like "us" from an Indonesian point of view. Except for "Chinese," the question of who is Indonesian in these cases seems not to have been debated.

Even in the memorialization of the revolution against the Dutch, it seems difficult for Indonesians to think that national violence was directed against those clearly not Indonesian. Here it is instructive to visit the army museum in Jakarta. The dioramas of the revolutionary struggle in this museum show the attacking Indonesian forces but very little of the Dutch enemy. By contrast, in a separate part of the museum, there are bloody shirts from slain Indonesian Muslims and other vivid reminders of the violence practiced against those who it is said betrayed the nation. It is hardly the case that Indonesia lacks xenophobia, but even when there are other identifications than Indonesian the word is still important in defining the target of aggression. And when Indonesian cannot be used to define the object of aggression, as with the Dutch whom one would expect to appear in the dioramas but do not, the enemy is simply not represented. One has the impression that Indonesians can only picture a victim of their lethal force if he replicates themselves.

Each act of large-scale violence raises up various specters from the history of the nation. The explanation of why Indonesians murder those like themselves has to take account of these specters. Here I will treat only one example, the massacres of so-called criminals in 1983 and 1984. At that time these people, most of them tattooed, were murdered by soldiers in mufti. Typically, Jeep-loads of masked, armed men drove to the homes of supposed criminals in the middle of the night, abducted them, repeatedly stabbed or shot them, and left the bodies on the streets or in rivers where they became spectacles.[1] This incident, though certainly the smallest among our list of Indonesian atrocities when one counts the number murdered, is especially important because in my opinion it shows how an idea of death existed that the state wanted to control. This notion was associated with the criminal, and the criminal, in turn, has a particular relation to the development of Indonesian nationalism.

The condition in which Indonesian nationalism arose was the development of the lingua franca of the Indies, Melayu, not only for commercial purposes, but for new forms of communication, especially newspapers and books. In this form, the same stories reached the major groups of the Indies. Many of these stories were translations of world literature. Some were stories that formerly were confined to separate ethnic groups because they were told only in the languages of that group. And some concerned criminals, especially thieves and murderers. The last were written by *meztisos* (children of Dutch fathers and women from the Indies) who, at the turn of the century, were in danger of losing their privileged relations with their Dutch fathers. In my interpretation, these stories were a way for meztisos to align themselves with the colonial power against criminals whom they pictured as "natives." The latter, they in effect said, were a menace to Dutch who remained unaware of the danger. In the evolution of anti-Dutch activities, "criminals" often played important roles, including during the revolutionary period.[2] One would think that nationalists would reevaluate these criminals, making them into nationalists or perhaps protonationalists. However criminals have rarely been included among the esteemed figures of history in Indonesian discourse.

The criminal, always on the edge of Indonesian society but never outside it, never the foreigner, has been available for Indonesian political discourse. Most recently he has been fit into the context of the notion of "the people," or *rakyat*. The word rakyat in many Indonesian societies referred to the followers of a leader. They were, first of all, retainers supported by those who had local political authority. In the context of nationalism the word evolved to mean the people. It referred, in different times and different contexts, to the audiences at political rallies and to those who associated themselves with the nationalist movement before the revolution. During the revolution, the relation of leaders to followers became problematic. The educated Indonesians who claimed to lead the revolution often had to be pushed into action by the youth who did the fighting. The cleavage between leaders and followers was marked by the thrust of some of the latter for a social revolution beyond the anticolonial struggle.[3]

With the achievement of independence, President Sukarno claimed to speak for the people in continuing the revolution. But from another perspective, when Sukarno spoke for the people, he integrated them into the state and thereby limited their social revolutionary impulses. It cannot be doubted, however, that a great many thought that their president spoke for them. When Sukarno was displaced and the New Order of President Suharto began, populist politics was put aside. "The people" became merely a term of reference; it was no longer a term of address, as it had been when Sukarno spoke to them in their own name. Since 1965, the people have lacked a voice to speak for them.

It was at that point, when the people had been suppressed, that a notion of criminality developed in Indonesia. Shortly after the change of regime, a newspaper called *Pos Kota* was started by supporters of the New Order, one of whose founders later became Minister of Information. The paper devotes itself almost exclusively to criminality. The news magazine *Tempo*, modeled on *Time* and also a New Order creation, had a rubric, *kriminalitas*, given over to crime and distinguished from other topics such as law and the nation. The criminals of kriminalitas, emerging from anonymity to cause discomforting surprise, were the continuation of "the people" adapted to the New Order. They came at a time when the division between classes has become increasingly marked by disparities in material conditions while explicit definitions of those who have and those who do not have are suppressed. It is a time when communication among various parts of the nation is felt to have been broken off, though this remains an implicit fear given the official thinking in which the nation is conceived of as a family while criticism is censored. "Criminals" are "the people" who, lacking a voice, burst onto the public scene nonetheless.

Communists and Criminals

Looking from the point of view of class, fear of communists had the same source as that of fear of criminals. Both sprang from the line drawn between the educated upper classes and those below that line. Such a statement is too general, not taking into account differences, for instance, between Muslims and leftists, or local social fissures that took less account of class differences. Nonetheless the criminals of 1983–1984 were not equated with communists. Criminality had its own history, separate from that of communists, although both resulted from the formation of the Indonesian nation rather than originating in local definitions. Not every element that emerged from the underside of the Indonesian national body was equated with every other element whose position it shares. Yet their common class definition would make such an equation expectable, particularly because, in my opinion, fear of revolution colors both words, "communist" and "criminal."

One might compare Indonesian violence to an intermittant civil war in which, by definition, members of the same nation kill each other. The 1948 battle and massacre—not war—between communists and nationalists approaches this. Yet the notion of vengeance complicates the comparison. In 1965, there was a widespread but certainly false belief that if communists had not been murdered, those who did the killing would have been their victims. This, along with the fear of communist vengeance in the years since then, seemed justified by the events of 1948. There is, however, no evidence at all that communists tried to take vengeance in 1965 for the events of 1948. Indeed, communists were widely expected to take power by constitutional means. Before they had the opportunity to do so, leading generals, some of their aides, and some of their family were murdered in a presumed coup attempt. Communists were blamed for the murder and accused of wanting to overthrow the regime. This justified killing them by the hundreds of thousands. But the motivation for the coup has remained unclear; scholars have doubted the role of the communists and even suggested that Suharto himself staged the presumed coup. In short, reliable evidence for vengeance on the part of communists does not exist.[4] But no one can doubt that since 1965 many Indonesians have feared communist revenge. Vengeance is not claimed by the murderers themselves; it is the one whom one kills, who, it is said, wants revenge.

The difficulty in thinking in terms of civil war or social revolution is that it presupposes a social division, such as that between brothers or between members of different classes, to which words such as communist and criminal refer. The odd place of vengeance complicates this reference. Instead of indicating a clear sociological and political position, communist and, in a different way, criminal, indicates to me something confused and even ghostly on the part of those dominant in the nation. Of course nothing precludes the victims from eventually generating a more political and sociological idea of vengeance, thus giving these terms a clearer sociological sense. But we speak of the classes that prevail. Certain fears haunt them, requiring various figures to account for them. One has to reach beyond class, however, to find the origins of these fears.

Since the 1980s at least, Indonesian political leaders have spoken of organizations without form when implying presumed communist resurgence. The state has gone to great lengths to keep track not only of those communists released from years in prison, but also of their descendants. This seems to indicate fear of something they cannot locate, even when they know precisely who is a communist and who is the son or daughter of one. Put differently, they cannot find a face or a name for their fears. The people they fear appear as ordinary and like themselves and, therefore, require more and more surveillance in order not to escape notice.[5]

One might think that those Indonesians today who fear vengeance are merely expressing guilt for their crimes. I believe there is an element of truth in this. But one would expect that guilt for a historical crime would be answered by survivors of that crime. One might expect there to be a culture of vengeance. But the survivors of the massacres of 1965 and 1966 have done very little to claim their own history. They have, for the most part, been content to reclaim their rights as Indonesian citizens, no different than their neighbors. There has been little, for instance, in the way of clandestine publishing.[6]

Perhaps for this reason, fear of retaliation has focused on imaginary enemies. The fear of communism is expressed as a fear of specters. There is a fear that the descendants of communists will take revenge for the murders of their parents and grandparents. "Evidence" for the murders is found in expressions of political discontent. So the regime bans historical novels on the grounds that they are "code books" used for indoctrination and that there exist organizations that have no form. Indonesians today think it necessary to respond to something they feel inhabits Indonesian society and that cannot be identified. Sometimes this fear is refracted through criminals, such as those massacred in 1983 and 1984, other times through communists, or still others.

The specters that inform Indonesian massacres vary from one time to the next. Even when one seems to reach a fundamental division between the people (the masses) and the elite (middle class), one cannot substitute one figure of the underclass for another. Not only does each have its particular historical development, but identifications of each are precarious. In the case of lower class criminals, for instance, no stereotyped visage has developed. Criminals appear in *Pos Kota* in small photographs, usually with a black bar across their eyes. One can find these same faces in other papers and magazines without the bar. One sees behind this photographically imposed mask or veil only the face of ordinary Indonesians. The face of the criminal does not reveal menace and evil. Rather, it mediates a realm of "death" (I put the word in quotes to indicate that it is not natural death but an Indonesian notion that is concerned), leading toward a force the state felt it lacked and which, in mastering the criminal, it hoped to have for itself. The face of the criminal is familiar, not strange, or, rather, strange in its familiarity.

It was his mediating role that made the criminal a target of state violence. The Indonesian criminal is, then, not an Other, different from oneself. His face, rather, is an object one sees through, as one sees through spectacles or telescopes. At the same time, given his historical determination, he is an Indonesian, a member of the same nation to which those who killed him belong or who, often enough, applauded his murder. He is a version of oneself who was either feared or envied because of his association with "death." Precisely because he is not different from oneself, what is his is potentially one's own. One can imagine standing in his place, as the forces of the Indonesian state do.

It should be evident that I see the idea of kriminalitas as part of the evolution of Indonesian political ideas. It is also important as such because it articulates the relations of an individual as he or she moves between family and nation. Earlier political notions functioned in the same way, developing with mass political participation. The first stirrings of what came to be Indonesian nationalism date from the end of the nineteenth century. Popular forms of participation, especially rallies, developed in the 1910s.[7] But truly massive participation in anticolonial politics did not occur until after World War II, when the Dutch colonizers, defeated by the Japanese, tried to reestablish the political control they had begun 300 years earlier. At that moment, enormous expectations were held by masses of Indonesians.

These expectations were embodied in certain words: *revolusi* (revolution), *merdeka* (freedom), Indonesia, and rakyat (the people). Such words served to conjoin individuals to the nation; their very pronounciation, particularly by such orators as Sukarno, could make people who otherwise would be sons, daughters, parents, farmers, merchants, or youth into members of the nation. It is my contention that "the people," in particular, formed a critical link in a symbolic chain that joined the family (and thus the region and the village) to the nation. Such words not only gave a nationalist status to those on whose behalf they were said. They also defined the relations of youth in regard to their parents and their regions. In chapter 1 I explain how this link was produced. Development, the equivalent word of the Suharto regime, is far less satisfactory in sustaining this linkage. Its relative failure left unfulfilled the urge for expression once filled by words such as revolusi, merdeka, rakyat, and a few others. Kriminalitas, introduced by the New Order, fills in the gap, though unsatisfactorily. That is, the urge to move out of the family into the nation in the New Order has the form of kriminalitas.

Kriminalitas is, in my opinion, the successor to the important political terms.[8] But I do not want to give the impression that kriminalitas occupies as central a place as either the people did once in Indonesia or as crime does in the United States. Most of the time, kriminalitas is mere diversion, comparable to *faits divers,* for which there is no exact English equivalent.[9] Dictionaries translate the term as "miscellaneous news items." But faits divers differ from the latter, as they are usually crime stories. The equivalent in U.S. tabloids includes the incredible: the world's longest zucchini, or "Satan Appears in Houston." Indonesian kriminalitas combines the two categories. The stories define the criminal as fantastic, even unbelievable. Such criminals are sensational but not memorable, exciting without being important. It is this nonmemorable character that I emphasize. Kriminalitas stories, unlike those of criminals of prenational times, rarely become part of cultural memory, though there are partial exceptions. Ordinarily, they claim only to be what people—other people—are talking about. And, indeed, that is their other important characteristic for us.

For the greater part of the time, kriminalitas seems to exist at the edge of memory. It eases its way into awareness, stimulating interest while somehow lacking significance and yet stretching credulity. But at the moment when the figures of kriminalitas, criminals, are massacred they enter explicit political awareness. Massacring them draws them into awareness; it is an attempt to make something that otherwise exists only hazily, but with implications of force, memorable, and to claim their power for the government. This is the moment when the new criminal type of Jakarta, the Indonesian state and its president, comes into view.

National Menace

On the one hand, Indonesians kill those they see to be in their own image. On the other, the targets of their murderous impulses have their own spectral histories, communists differing from criminals, for instance. But behind the faces of communists and criminals there is in common a sense of menace, the origins of which cannot be securely located in historical events but must be looked for in the cultural formations just sketched. That there is more than one figure of the menace inherent in Indonesia could indicate different sources for different menaces. Or it could indicate that whatever the source of national menace, no figure adequately represents it. Whichever the case, the threat is located in the faces of ordinary persons, people not substantially different from those of other Indonesians who govern them.

It is the commonality of visage that made a notion of power accessible to the officials of the state, producing a new criminal type. To the state the menace was an attraction. It was the lethal power that the state wanted for its own. It is my thesis that the state itself took on the form of a criminal in order to obtain this power. The result was the contrary of the cases already mentioned. The massacres of Hutus and Tutsis or Serbs and Croats are between peoples deeply involved with each other. In these massacres people similar to each other strove to make each the other. Following a process that has been described often in many places, one might say that they tried to make a part of themselves foreign in order to expel it and leave themselves ethnically "pure." In the case of Indonesian criminals, by contrast, the state imitated the criminal, striving to become like him. In the process, a new understanding of "death" arose, one with a national rather than local or familial context. It is this that I call the nationalization of "death."

1 Illegitimacy and "The People"

*In the Adat [customary] law even an illegitimate child can
become an heir.*
—Kijaji R. H. Moh. Adnan

In his *Autobiography: As Told to Cindy Adams* (Jakarta: Gunung Agung,
1965) President Sukarno speaks of his youth; he tells how poor his family
was.[1] His father could not afford a midwife. Then he leaps forward in time
to speak of the rumor about his birth that circulated after he became
prominent and that one could still hear in 1965. He says they say:

> "He is the illegitimate son of a Dutch planter who made love with a
> native peasant in the field, then farmed the baby out for adoption."
>
> Unfortunately the only witness to swear to my real father and to
> testify that I did, indeed, come from my true mother, not some coffee
> worker in the field, had long since passed away. (18–19)

It is a question of his parentage and, therefore, of his legitimacy. The story
was told by the Dutch in order to claim him for themselves and thus, no
doubt, to show that an opponent who could defeat them must be one of
them, not a mere "native." For the Dutch who told this story, at least,
Sukarno is an illegitimate Dutchman. It is a strange sort of racism that
denies the Other by making him one of their own.

The story, as I remember, could be heard without much trouble in
Dutch circles. But it was more widespread than that, being told also in
Jakarta among certain Indonesians in the 1960s. It is interesting to speculate for a moment on the idea that the first president of the Republic of
Indonesia was illegitimate. Sukarno was, in a sense, the father of the nation. The scandal, of course, is that somehow the legitimacy of the nation
and the legitimacy of the president would be confused.

Mixing the legitimacy of the state and the legitimacy of the person of its president is perhaps not entirely an accident. At least that is the suggestion when one sees that in his own autobiography (also as-told-to),[2] President Suharto concerns himself at great length with the same issue. But it takes him a while to reach it:

> I have to clarify my genealogy because there is someone who wrote a falsehood in October, 1974 in a certain magazine. I ordered Dipo (G. Dwipayana) to refute this piece of writing and to circulate [the refusal] in the magazines and newspapers published in Jakarta. But a day later I ordered reporters to the Palace to my office. I wanted to clarify my genealogy myself. In front of reporters both from abroad and not, I explained that I had no noble blood. (6)

One would think that this false notion would not stimulate so much concern on the part of someone who had the affairs of the nation to take care of, particularly because it would seem only to enhance him. But not only did Suharto himself "personally" (as he emphasized) make the denial, he produced what he termed witnesses:

> I presented to this collection of reporters several old people, witnesses, still living, who were well familiar with my genealogy. I am the descendant of Bapak Kertosudiro alias Kertogejo, *ulu-ulu* [village irrigation official] who himself did not own an inch of rice field. (6–7)

Suharto, like Sukarno, insists on his poverty, a topic to which I shall return. He is not proud of his poverty as, for instance, a U.S. politician might be. It does not indicate that he worked his way up, that he is responsible for his success himself. It is, rather, a source of shame. He writes apropos of the poverty of his parents:

> I will be frank: in facing life when I was small, I suffered much that others perhaps never experienced. (7)

He confesses his poverty because it is the truth of his descent. If he is credited with noble birth, it would be dangerous. There would be a risk he feels he cannot take.

> I told them, these false written reports about my genealogy could be misinterpreted or could be used as ammunition for those who want not only to hurt me but my family and forefathers and perhaps also the Indonesian state and nation. (7)

We have reached the point where the state and the person of the president are confounded, this time explicitly. The problem with being called

"noble" when it is untrue is that it could be misinterpreted. There is only
one direction this misinterpretation would take:

> At the very least I believe that this false report could make people start
> to ask questions and could confuse them. In fact, this President now,
> what exactly is his descent? (8)

Once people start to wonder about the genealogy of the president, there is
no way to control what they will think and say:

> If a for and against arises, automatically each one will defend his own
> position and there could be controversy. (7)

The problem with controversy is that it makes trouble:

> This could be a good opportunity for those who engage in subversion
> and carry out guerrilla activities, and could disturb national stabil-
> ity. (8)

Suharto imagines that given the opportunity, others will think about his
birth. The result is that, rather than be impressed by the favorable but
untrue information already disseminated in the Indonesian press, diversity of opinion would arise. This would damage not only him, his family,
and his ancestors, but the nation itself. It would provoke guerrilla action and the nation could be destabilized. It is an extraordinary train of
thought and it does not end there:

> In fact, we are in great need of national stability in order to develop.
> And I think there is even more. If this writing is true, it shows that a
> boy of 6 was given away by his mother just like that to a friend in
> Kemusuk Village. This pictures a woman without [moral] value.
> Automatically conflict between men and women will appear in this
> business of evaluation. This too can give a picture of an undesirable
> situation. Maybe an impression even worse than that can arise; why
> would a wife give away a child so young, only 6 years old; perhaps
> because the marriage wasn't valid. (7)

We have reached the point of illegitimacy again. And, once again, this
illegitimacy will damage the nation.

> Thus, if invalid [speaking of the marriage], an illegitimate child, a
> bastard. Wouldn't that stain the name of the nation and the state? (7)

Of course, unlike the case of Sukarno, nothing occurred. There is no
gossip about Suharto's illegitimate birth, at least so far as he acknowledges.

It is rather that, as he says in the following sentences, he "looks to the future" when this gossip might arise with the result that not only his "private name" [sic], his ancestors, but him "as the person who by chance has gained the trust of the people (rakyat) to be president. . . ." I cannot finish the sentence because of Suharto's garbled syntax, but he explains that "writing like that" will be, once more, material for subversion and political guerrillas. "Because of that my genealogy has to be made clear." (8)

Illegitimacy is connected with the nation, with nationalism, and with the state. In both instances it is also connected with gossip. There seems to be no actual illegitimacy; it is merely hearsay, but, it is feared, widely circulated hearsay. It is for that reason that it is harmful to "the nation and the state" according to Suharto. He is not explicit about how this would damage the state; presumably because the people would lose confidence in him. But more is involved than that because, as I have said, he does not hear gossip; he starts simply from having read a piece about his parentage that attributes noble birth to him. When he sees his name in print and sees that he has been attributed a father who was not actually his own father, he pictures people gossiping. And when he pictures gossip, he invents what they will say and finds "them" revising his own past. National security being at stake, he sets the record straight, not only ordering an aide to do so, but doing so himself, summoning witnesses, and so on.

This is a lot of effort to head off a possibility that he seems to be the first to have envisioned. It makes one want to look further into the relation of the nation, the president, illegitimacy, and gossip. To find out more about how these connections are made we can turn back to President Sukarno. Sukarno was born of a Balinese mother and a Javanese father. He considered precisely this mixture to be typically Indonesian:

> Through generations, Indonesian blood has mixed with the Indian, Arab, some pure Polynesian strain and, of course, Chinese. We are basically a Malay tribe. From the root of *Ma* comes Manila, Madagascar, Malaya, Madura, Maori, Himalaya. Our ancestors migrated across Asia, settled in 3,000 islands and became Balinese, Javanese, Atjehnese, Ambonese, Sumatran, and so forth. (19)

It is this mixture that defines "Indonesian"; but it is a mixture that leaves out Dutch and European. This omission is not a question of when Malay identity was formed, which might exclude the Dutch on grounds of their late arrival. But although they are not exactly coterminous with Arabs and Chinese, the Dutch arrived at nearly the same time as large numbers of Chinese.

Mixture is a source of legitimacy just so long as Europeans are not included. One might attribute this question of legitimacy to the Dutch practice of taking concubines in the Indies and the fact that acknowledgment by the father of his offspring conferred the civil status of Dutch, leaving those with Dutch fathers who refused to acknowledge them as bastards and with the civil status of their mothers ("Javanese" for instance).[3] But even those children of mixed European and "native" couples who did not marry could acquire the status European by being acknowledged by their fathers. Paternity was linked to nation in the oldest senses of that term, by multiple means. But this meant as well that for some, nationality could indicate illegitimacy of birth. It is this, of course, that the Dutch relied on in claiming Sukarno as one of their own by his paternity while at the same time denying him because of the illegitimacy of that paternity. The same questions might arise with the birth of a child from, for instance, a Javanese mother and a Minangkabau or a Chinese father. But with the rise of nationalism precisely this possibility was legitimated while European parentage continued to imply illegitimacy. Sukarno's response to gossip that no doubt originated in the Dutch community, was to state that his father was Javanese, his mother Balinese, and to claim the very mixture as a new possibility indicating a certain protonationalism.

No sooner does Sukarno make the claim for legitimacy based on the identity of his father and mother than he implicitly raises the question of legitimacy again, this time, and more strangely, because of his mother. Sukarno's mother's father refused the request of Sukarno's father to marry his daughter. "We'll lose our daughter," Sukarno reports him as saying. So they eloped. And, Sukarno adds, elopement is part of the tradition of Balinese marriage. But:

> Balinese elopement follows strict rules. Elopers spend their wedding night in the home of friends while couriers are dispatched to the bride's parents to inform them their daughter is now married. Mother and father sought refuge with the Javanese chief of police who was a friend of father's. Mother's family came to take her back, but the Police Chief said, "No, she's under my protection."
>
> It is not our habit to haul a groom into court, but those were unusual circumstances. After all, he was a Javanese Muslim Theosophist and she a Balinese Hindu-Buddhist. When the case came up, Mother was asked, "Did this man force you against his will?" And Mother replied, "Oh no. I loved him and eloped because I wanted to."
>
> There was no choice but to allow the marriage. Nonetheless, the

court fined mother 25 seringget [sic], the equivalent of $25. Mother had inherited several gold bracelets and to pay the money she sold the ornaments.

Rightfully feeling unloved in Bali, Father applied to the Department of Education for a transfer to Java. He was sent to Surabaya and there I was born." (21; end of chapter one)

What makes Sukarno's parents legitimately married, it seems, is that they followed the wedding customs of his mother's people. But there was a certain irregularity, indicated by the fine they had to pay. As I understand Balinese *adat,* a couple can marry by elopement but, as Sukarno pointed out, they have to inform the bride's parents within a few days. Before that time, her parents can reclaim her. In this case, it seems that the custom was not strictly followed. It was, nonetheless, allowed by the colonial court. And allowed on the basis of a theme of nationalist stories: love. "Oh no. I loved him and eloped because I wanted to," are the words Sukarno puts into his mother's mouth as she speaks to the judge.

Love, justifying marriage by the consent of the couple even against the wishes of parents, is a theme of nationalist novels, particularly Sumatran ones, from the 1920s and 1930s. There are two effects of this love. First, the authority of parents is strictly limited. It is against their wishes that a Javanese marries a Balinese. But this coupling furthers the mixture of peoples that composes the Indonesian nation. If it is counter to one set of norms, regional or local ones, it is, nonetheless, still legitimate because it is in keeping with another set. The love of nationalists in novels is always legitimate. It ends either in marriage or, in the earlier novels in particular, in the death of the couple, or of at least one of them, because they cannot suffer that norms be broken. Nationalism and love are linked because through it, peoples are mixed and a new authority is claimed. The authority of the family is claimed by the nation. Still, this claim to a national authority ensured morality was made against an earlier, familial claim. Conflict with parental authority no doubt informed the feeling of susceptibility to being thought illegitimate of Sukarno and, we shall see, other nationalists.

I have tried to demonstrate elsewhere that the morality of nationalist love upheld against familial authority not only reclaimed familial authority for the nation but made Europeans the locus of immorality, displacing to their continent and those people the sexual freedom that might otherwise have gone into the making of the nation. As it was, the making of the Indonesian nation was a double process: the mixing of peoples we have seen, and the exclusion of some peoples, a sort of early form of not ethnic but national cleansing. Were love to be what it was in eighteenth-century France, the course of nationalism, if not the revolution, might have been different.

Family and Nation

At the beginning of this chapter is a quote taken from the transcript of a conversation on 22 July 1940, between the advisor for native affairs of the Dutch East Indies and the leader of an organization of Islamic judges.[4] The Dutch had revised the court system giving preference to traditional systems of inheritance over Islamic law. K. H. Adnan was an opponent of these changes. He had many arguments but the one quoted, that according to traditional law even illegitimate children could inherit, was perhaps the most deeply felt. Of course, from the point of view of indigenous societies, the children considered illegitimate would not necessarily be so. The cases most troublesome for the Islamic judges were those when a child was taken into the household and afterwards became an heir even though there was no formal adoption. It seems to be this that K. H. Adnan referred to in his statement. This conflict of legitimacies is only apparent in retrospect. Before the claim by Islam, the heir would think he was entitled to what he received. Afterwards he might think that the person whom he called father was not really his father, and that he himself was, somehow, illegitimate even if all of his experience said the opposite.

That is more or less the case with Indonesian nationalists. With them it was not usually a question of inheritance but, as I have said, of the right of parents to chose marriage partners for their children. It was in the name of another law that the authority of parents was abridged without being outlawed entirely. Nationalist activity brought a sense of solidarity to peoples who before did not feel solidarity as marked by intermarriage. Even within a single group it also created a new authority allowing freedom of choice of marriage partners. The sense of illegitimacy was created precisely because a new legitimacy was pronounced. Like Islam, nationalism intruded on traditional societies in Indonesia. Its force was, in part, derived from its intrusive quality, which is to say that in local terms it was ununderstandable. Parents, for instance, were scandalized to think that they were no longer to control marriage choices of their progeny. They looked for marriage partners in the interest of the family including their children; they felt innocent of wrong doing. And yet they were labeled unenlightened by standards that began not as illumination but as something perhaps desirable but not entirely comprehensible. Even young nationalists tended to believe in the forces of enlightenment and nationalism rather than to understand them. The binding quality of nationalism, its ability to make itself felt as right and as obligatory, was tied to the sense that it was something other than one knew, that nothing within traditional society prepared one for it.[5]

Once a nationalist, in retrospect, parental authority seemed arbitrary and worse. Nationalist authority did not replace the father. Instead it made him a nationalist product. It in fact strengthened the impression of paternal power in one direction while weakening it in another. Early nationalist novels and nationalist biographies are filled with pictures of weak fathers and tyrannical parents. Tyrannical precisely in the limitations they placed on their children, tyrannical when placed alongside nationalist idealism and notions of love (*cinta*), but weak whenever they were pictured alongside colonial authority. By contrast, the good father, both powerful and moral, was the nationalist leader.[6]

From this perspective, looking back, the family in which one was raised is put into question. From the point of view of Islam, tradition does not produce law; it produces *adat* or customary ways of behaving, ways that are historical, geographical, and cultural accretions. They have a claim to the degree that they do not conflict with the syariah (Islamic law). But these ways are not 'law'. They do not have the imperative quality of law. From the point of view of nationalism, the same is true. Familial ways were customary rather than legal. The notion of incest was never challenged; but if one reads the novels of the conflict of adat and nationalism current in the 1920s and 1930s the effect of nationalism was to loosen desire only to put it to nationalist ends.

The school teacher or another nationalist authority took the place of the parent in guiding lovers into moral behavior that differed from traditional morality only in the choice of partner. Familial authority was thus coopted by nationalists. Indonesian nationalism was more than a political program directed against colonialism; it was a movement of authority from the family to the nation. It is again this movement that produced feelings of illegitimacy. After the fact, familial authority was put in doubt. If parents continued to be honored, it was partly because familial authority was never renounced and partly because it refounded itself on a nationalist basis. The authority of parents was strengthened as well as weakened. But it was strengthened because the justification for familial authority was placed outside the family. The Indonesian, as opposed to the customary family, based itself on an assumption of morality that was both universally rational and national. This morality was all the stronger for being assumed to be enlightened without being the topic of debate.

Nationalist uneasiness about the traditional family took the form of doubt about the law that informed it. Parents themselves no longer embodied the law; did they obey it? How could they when before the nation came into being they did not know it? It is here that one can place the familiar theme of the lack of enlightenment of traditional ways of Indonesian nationalism, which was equated with modernity. What had been customary seen from the perspective of nationalism lost its legitimating force and displayed itself as the workings of desire. Adherence to new authority, new law, left the suspicion that the old ways were illegitimate. And it is these old ways in which one was produced.

After the fact, the traditional family is suspected of being outside the law. But attitudes were ambivalent and parents remained respected, more often pitied than condemned. This was sometimes the case even when they were accused of arbitrariness in the choice of their children's marriage partners. The presidents of Indonesia defended their parents, but in their arguments one senses that they themselves understood that their parents, particularly Suharto's, were vulnerable to suspicions of behaving illegitimately because they were "backward natives." The cases differ. Sukarno's father was a school teacher, thus less vulnerable to accusations of backwardness than Suharto's. But here it is important to note that the accusers Sukarno concerned himself with were the Dutch, who from Sukarno's perspective were likely to assimilate his father to the colonial stereotype of the backward native. His mother's defense, as reported by Sukarno, that she loved his father, is his assertion of their modernity, hence their enlightenment and their morality. Parental vulnerability to suspicion implies doubt about the capacities of fathers and mothers to know proper ways, leaving these presidents worried about what people— and themselves, it is clear—think about their origins.[7]

But there is another perspective from which to see the relation of family and nation. Though I see doubt about familial authority and morality as an effect of nationalism, I also believe this doubt has a nationalist solution. Nationalist thought offered a link between family and nation that founded itself on what one might call the natural immorality of the family and which transformed what in every family would develop into incest into a way to both remove oneself from parents, especially mothers, and keep them in respectful memory.

Let us return to Sukarno's account of his childhood. Poverty, in the discourse of the time, was exclusion. But, Sukarno claimed, the poverty of his family was different:

> Our kind of poverty makes for closeness. When there was nothing material, when it seemed I had nothing in the whole world but Mama, I clung to her because she was my sole satisfaction; she was the candy I couldn't have and she was all my worldly possessions. Oh, Mama had a heart so big. (23)

Impoverished Sukarno has another source of riches, of luxury even, namely his mother. His father has only a negative importance; he leaves a place open for Sukarno's mother to love him. Sukarno is indebted to her not only for bringing him into the world and for the necessities of his life, but also precisely for the riches, the "candy," the luxury she gave him. She is a source from whom he got not only himself but even more than that. Sukarno's mother is a magician of a sort; she transforms poverty into wealth.

Sukarno owes her everything. But still to respond to her was something he apparently had to learn or at least to be reminded about. There was another figure in the house, a woman called Sarinah.

> Sarinah was part of our household. Unmarried, she was to us a member of the family. She got no wages whatsoever. She it is who taught me to love. Sarinah taught me to love people. Masses of people. While she cooked in the small shed outside the house, I'd sit with her and she'd preach, "Karno, over and above everybody you must love your mother. But then you must love the small people. You must love humanity." Sarinah is a common name, but this was not a common woman. She was the greatest single influence of my life. (25)

His family was poor, but as John Legge points out, it was poor like most Javanese but not impoverished within the context of Java.[8] Poverty, as Sukarno uses it here, is a term of comparison between Dutch and Javanese and not within Javanese society. It marks the exclusion of Javanese. But in that excluded realm there is another sort of riches, his mother and her gifts. She is at the origin not only of Sukarno himself, but of a social realm outside the restrictions of colonial society. He, Sukarno, has a permanent debt to his mother, even more, perhaps, than most people do to theirs, because she offers a certain political possibility. Or rather, she is at the source of a political possibility.

Sukarno has to learn to love in return for the love of his mother. This return is linked to love of the people. Sarinah marks this linkage. It is Sarinah who taught him to love his mother and, in the next sentence, to love the people. Further, Sarinah was his mother's aide and in that capacity also her substitute. She fed Sukarno, she was member of the family. As he describes her she is a substitute for his mother; like her she gives. But she was also more than that:

> In my young days we shared the same narrow cot. When I had grown up a little, there was no Sarinah anymore. I filled the void by sleeping with Sukmini [his older sister] in the same bed. Later I slept with our dog Kiar, who was mixture of fox terrier and something Indonesian— I don't know exactly what. Moslems supposedly don't like dogs, but I adore them. (25)

"Sarinah" is not only someone who fills in for his mother, she is the first in a chain of substitutions. She teaches him to make further ones later and still to keep a profound relation to his mother. After Sarinah, there are other substitutes for his mother, but Sarinah is both the first and the one that makes substitution possible, all the while keeping Sukarno in touch with his origins.

Sukarno, in relation to Sarinah, is also in relation to his mother and, after her, to others: his sister and even his dog. He sleeps with them all. As we will see, this does not end the series. In one regard, there is nothing unusual about this story from an Indonesian point of view, except for the dog. The dog, as Sukarno himself says, is exceptional. As the exception, it simply shows how far the series of those with whom Sukarno sleeps extends. The dog represents a principal of inclusion. Sukarno is close to beings one would never suspect. But it is Sarinah who has a special place. She has a double role. It is through her that Sukarno learns to respond and to respond in the special way called love. Through her he learns he has a debt that cannot be repaid and that he must, nonetheless, continually try to repay. And as we have seen, she is the first of those who substitute for his mother; the first in a series that continues further than Sukarno notes in his conversation with Cindy Adams.

The series consists of those with whom he is close, that is, those to whom he responds in the sense that he pays attention to them and is fond of them. His response is disinterested in the sense that he gets nothing material back from the attention he pays them. But at the same time, he owes them something. His affection is a sign of debt, a return for the affection they give him. They give him affection; they share his bed, which is a deeper sharing even than if it were a sexual act. That would be perverse. This is not perverse; it creates or deepens a social bond of which anyone must approve. But if there is no perversion here it is because there is substitution. He sleeps first with his mother, then others take her place. The ability to substitute is the guarantee of morality. It is a series that continues in the register of gratefulness and comes to include "the people." It is, finally, in the political register that Sukarno repays his debt to his mother; he comes to love the people. Sukarno revises his relation to his mother in retrospect. Without the intervention of Sarinah Sukarno risked remaining enclosed in his family, tied always to his mother in a suspicious way. With Sarinah, his relation to his mother is transformed; it is a question of indelible and respectful memory; he forgets nothing he received from her and all that he received was symbolically rich. It is an idealization that transforms what otherwise would be ambiguous.

Sukarno's parents were legally married. Yet if he committed incest it would raise the question of his illegitimacy. He would still be the son of his father, but his mother would be something more or something less than his mother. His very being would be corrupt. It is precisely in lieu of bestiality and incest, and by means of substitution, that another place to which he must respond is marked. This place to which he must answer is that occupied by "the people." There is a double question of law involved: first is the avoidance of bestiality and incest, that is of sexual crimes; second is the forging of a social bond through inclusion. One that, in the continuity of its generalization, includes those who otherwise, in the struggle for the nation before independence (and even after) would have no legal status: the rakyat, or the people.

Before turning to the relation between Sukarno and the people, let us give one more thought to Sukarno's potential criminality. Were he to have committed incest or bestiality, he would be a criminal. But, again, he is a criminal not necessarily by standards of national law but by what is thought to be a natural law that transcends even family or customary law. His crime would be fundamental. Imagine as the first president of the republic someone who committed incest. Were he somehow to make incest acceptable, it would certainly strike at the very basis of differentiation within the family. But one might imagine a nation composed of people even more tightly bound to one another because they were tied by the multiple bonds incest alone makes possible. It would be a nation like no other. It would be what anthropologists of another era called a hoard. This, indeed, is close to what Sukarno envisioned for the nation.

The Extension of the Tongue of the People

It was President Sukarno's custom to give an address each year on the 17th of August, the day on which independence was proclaimed. In 1963, the speech was given in the vast new stadium called Gelora Bung Karno, the Turbulence of Bung Karno. The address touched on topics of neocolonialism: continuation of the policy of Confrontation with Malaysia, support for the Games of the New Emerging Forces, and improvement of the economy, which was in disarray. The date of 17 August 1963 was yet another occasion on which he explained how he became the "extension of the tongue of the people." He did so in the context of the Economic Declaration or *Dekon*, which he saw as a way of escaping from control of the great powers. Addressing himself to the donors of aide, he said,

> Our economy will be Indonesian . . . and will be securely founded on our own cultural and spiritual heritage. That heritage may be fertilized by assistance from beyond the seas, but its fruits and flowers will be our own. Thus, please do not expect that any forms of assistance will produce a mirror image of yourself."

Sukarno believed he could escape foreign control if he acted in a way that was purely Indonesian and purely revolutionary. He found this way, he said, by listening to the voice of the people.

> I am now paying full attention to the voice of the people with regard to the execution of *Dekon*. I have often said . . . that I am merely the extension of the tongue of the People. When I am convinced of the genuine voice of the common people, then, God willing, my own tongue gives sound to the conscience of the common people.

The question is how he became convinced of the genuineness of the people's voice. How, that is, he claimed to hear it in order to respond to it. And in this case to respond in order to escape the coercion of the great world powers. It was on the birthday of the nation that he found the means to become the extension of the tongue of the people.

> At present I am not in the first place speaking as President Mandatary, or as President/Prime Minister, as President/Supreme Commander—I speak here as the Extension of the Tongue of the People of Indonesia—as President Great Leader of the Revolution.

On these birthdays of the nation Sukarno identified himself fully with the people. He was not only an extension of their collective body, he was also that body divided in two, thus able to be apart from them, but only in order better to hear them and to speak with them:

> In every Seventeenth of August meeting . . . it is as though I held a dialogue. A dialogue with the People. A two-way conversation be-

> tween Sukarno-the-man and Sukarno-the-People, a two-way conver-
> sation between comrade in arms and comrade in arms. A two-way
> conversation between two comrades who in reality are One. . . . That
> is why, every time I prepare a Seventeenth of August address . . . I
> become like a person possessed.

Sukarno, as "extension of the tongue of the people," is also Sukarno-the-
People. He speaks with himself; he is the people. And at the same time he is
as though "possessed by the people." It would be easier to comprehend
him if we changed the order: because he is possessed by the people, it is as
though between him and them there is no difference. It is by this means
that he projects himself to become "the extension of the tongue of the
people."

When independence day comes, in the stadium in front of Sukarno are
the people, the rakyat. These people form a part of the rest of the Indonesian people, not present in the stadium, but equally present to President
Sukarno:

> I am standing before the Indonesian people—face to face. . . . The
> Indonesian people, both those who are gathered here in this stadium,
> those through out the whole of Indonesia via the media of radio and
> television, as well as those abroad, also via the media of radio and
> television.

Distance does not separate him from the rakyat, thanks to radio and
television, which bring his voice to them. But it is also because the people
exist not as sociological beings but precisely as those he imagines to be his
audience and the source of his energy and his message. The people, then,
are not constructed for him out of actual communications, but as a result
of imagining communications, those that reach him and those he relays;
"the people" are both the source of what he says and one of his addressees.

But this formulation is not quite correct because Sukarno, as extension
of the tongue of the people, is already confounded, in his mind, with the
people. There is a certain confusion of tongues, we might say, when his
tongue is theirs. The possibility of this confusion is also the possibility of
representing the people. Through it, he knows what the people want, who
they are; and through the energy he derives from them he articulates what
they cannot articulate for themselves. "The people," says Sukarno, are "my
brothers and sisters whose tongues cannot speak for themselves." That
being the case, "I must formulate all our ideas, crystallize all our ideas,
condense all our ideas." This is what is meant by being "the extension of

the tongue of the people." The energy, the impetus to speak comes from the people. The formulation comes from Sukarno.

But if Sukarno articulates, he insists that the origin rests with the people. Not just as energy, impetus, or, one might say, "inspiration." The people are more than a muse. They control his voice. The title of Sukarno's 1963 speech on the birthday of the nation was "The Resounding Voice of the Indonesian Republic" (*Genta Suara Republik Indonesia*). Genta, the word in the official translation that is rendered as "resounding voice" literally means bell, as in "cowbell." The sense of the phrase is that the republic makes itself heard in the way that a bell does. If there is any message conveyed by this ringing it is at most an alarm or a summoning of attention in the way that a cowbell lets the owner know the whereabouts of his cow.

Sukarno, describing himself as this vibrating voice, goes further. He shows how he himself vibrates on the occasion of his communion with the people:

> Everything invisible in my body seethes (or overflows); my thoughts seethe, my feelings seethe, my nerves seethe, my emotions seethe. Everything unseen in my body then vibrates, becomes spirited and shakes and for me, fire is as though it is not hot enough, the sea is not deep enough, the stars in the heavens are not high enough.

The verbs used for vibrate and shake are active as well as passive, thus making Sukarno vibrate as a result of his communion and making him also the cause of further vibrations that, ultimately, form the sounds of his voice as it travels to the people, just as it traveled from the people.

Sukarno's annual communion, his night with the people one might say, serves an essential purpose. The messages formed and transmitted assure the identity of the Indonesian people. In 1963, for instance, it meant that economic aid would not mean their subservience to foreign powers or their becoming a "mirror image" of anything foreign.

His message, through the power of radio and television, reaches not only the people:

> I am standing before the Indonesian people—face to face. . . . And I am aware, too, that on every 17th of August I am also facing the outside world which is not Indonesian, whether as a friend facing a friend, or as enemy facing enemy.

These two pictures of himself, as having a source in the people and as articulating and broadcasting to them and for them, recur throughout the speech.

As for his Indonesian audience, one knows that they did, in a way, "seethe" in his presence. One knows their enthusiasm at the time. There can be no doubt that many of them assumed that Sukarno spoke for them. Those who did so were aware of the pressing economic difficulties of the time. They were likely to be less sure of what Sukarno meant in his speech by "revolutionary economics," a term he contrasted with the technical economics practiced by experts. But, hearing him, if they thought he spoke for them, they were in agreement with his notion. But they could not have had his ideas in mind when they entered the stadium, so it is difficult to speak of agreement. After the fact, after his expression, they must have thought that what he said is what they meant all the time.

But just as Sukarno was confounded by the people, the people were confounded with Sukarno. Such confusion was possible only when rakyat ceased to mean what it did originally: the following of a political leader, the persons this leader supported, and who owed him allegiance. This was a sociological notion, which, even if it might sometimes be blurred at its boundaries, always had a material expression. But rakyat as Sukarno used it was different. No one was a member of the rakyat by virtue of a prior sociological distinction. Farmers (*petani*), for instance, were so not because they were farmers but because (and when) they were pronounced to be members of the rakyat by a nationalist leader. Rakyat was a word in a performative utterance; the people existed because the word was said and did not exist before that. One might, for instance, argue that the rakyat, being seldom pronounced, scarcely exist in Indonesia under the New Order, the period after Sukarno was forced out of the presidency, though there were still plenty of farmers.

In Sukarno's time the word rakyat was performative, the remarkable linguistic phenomenon that brings what is uttered into existence. An example would be a promise.[9] It is Sukarno in particular who executed this performance. But as I have already suggested, his utterance was linked in his own mind to an earlier place in which Sarinah was critical as the figure that taught him to love, that is, the place from which he constantly received riches, even in the midst of poverty, just as he received messages, energy, the possibility of articulation from the people despite the great poverty of Indonesia in 1963. Sarinah was also the first substitute, thus critical in finding further substitutive forms, ending in rakyat. These substitutes were always traceable back to their origin, the source of what he constantly received: his mother. One can say that through the possibility of having replacements for her, which range from Sarinah first of all to the rakyat, Sukarno guarded his access to a source of riches that were only figural; that is to say, to language.

The rakyat in Sukarno's speech were as much a displacement as a substitute. They thus remained charged with some of the same erotic component that informed Sukarno's early relations. Perhaps it was not only for political reasons then that, when Suharto took power from President Sukarno in 1966, he ended the period of populist politics that depended on the rakyat. But by that time, the word was critical in regulating the relation between family and nation. In its place was a return to conventional notions of father as sources of authority responsible for the installation of morality in the family. But to date this has never entirely freed itself from reliance on a national morality. Nor has the infusion of the state with familial rubrics, especially paternal ones, and the creation of long lines of patronage culminating in the person of the president fully absorbed the charge that passed through Sukarno's speech.[10] The consequences of breaking the symbolic chain from mother to rakyat have not been fully brought under control. It is a linguistic or literary question of the formation of figural language and of feeling the force tending toward figural expression when such production does not take place.[11]

In asserting his authority, Sukarno produced the rakyat. When the figure of the people is given up, one replacement is simply the anonymous mass who spread rumors. These rumors are precisely the fears assuaged by and for Sukarno when he becomes the extension of the tongue of the people. Speaking for the rakyat, familial crime is transformed into politically potent communicative power. Without the rakyat and the possibility of speaking for them, there is no control of this power. Instead, with Suharto, there is gossip far more menacing than the gossip about Sukarno. It menaces the state and even the nation. We have seen Suharto's strange and extravagant fear on this score. Suharto first imagines people gossiping about his parentage, then thinks of the controversy that might arise from such gossip, and finally fears that political guerrillas will destabilize the state. We are not far from the criminals of kriminalitas. The criminal of kriminalitas is a figure functionally equivalent to the menacing guerrilla-gossipers. He, too, arises in the absence of the rakyat as the attempt to fill in the gap between familial origins and national identity. And he, too, is attributed the possession of a powerful communicative power that threatens Indonesia.

In chapter 4 of this study I discuss the government's massacre of supposed criminals in the 1980s. Here I want to anticipate this account in order to illustrate a fundamental component of kriminalitas. The great bulk of the murdered criminals were men with tattoos. The papers seldom identified the victims by their criminal past but rather by their markings. Headlines such as this appeared in *Pos Kota* in 1982.

> Edi, covered with tattoos, murdered. His head wounded and his neck twisted.

The story of Edi consists of not much more than this:

> The written words Edi Basri are possibly the name of this man. There were also the written words Dasri and the name Santi. It is not clear to what these refer. The whole of the rest of his body was covered with pictures of various sorts. (29 October 1983)

Most of the time, the papers simply noted that the bodies were tattooed without giving their nature. Tattoos were traditionally marks of bandit gangs. But these tattoos were not secret signs. They were usually names of the bearer, of lovers, or they were pictures, often of women, or sometimes inscriptions. They did not ordinarily indicate criminals. Indeed, after a few months, men who claimed never to have had criminal pasts but who simply were tattooed began to turn themselves into the police out of fear of being murdered. The targeting of tattooed men, always accused of criminality and almost never of specific crimes, gives us an indication of kriminalitas as presented by journalists.

In one case, described under the headline "Two tattooed men shot" (4 November 1983), one of the murdered men is described as bearing the inscription, "There is no use weeping for the death of a scoundrel" (Tiada guna kau tangiskan kematian seorang bajingan). This tattoo is quite formal in its language. In my translation this might appear as the boast of someone dedicated to the elimination of scoundrels, meant to be displayed to a potential victim. But in Indonesian, the reader is addressed directly. One could retranslate the phrase this way: "There is no point for you in weeping for the death of a scoundrel." The suggestion is that the reader is present and that it is the death of the bearer of the tattoo that is inscribed. The phrase suggests that the writing is meant to outlast the person who displayed it. It is his epitaph. But it is highly improbable that it was made to be read by the man's murderer. It is much more likely to have been addressed to a lover or a potential lover. In that case it would be a sort of advertisement of the person inscribed. He presents himself as already gone, creating pathos for himself that was meant for those he would like to have be fond of him.

But at the same time, the speaker is dignified and does not use his ordinary voice. It is an authority who speaks, one who transcends fear of death and who acknowledges it at the same time as the decisive moment in the construction of his own memory. It could be an inscription on a tombstone.

Meant for a lover, when it appears in the newspaper, the context is not love but criminality and politics. His body is bared now to his murderers and to newspaper readers. With this warping of contexts the message gains more strength than it could ever possibly have had during the man's amorous adventures. Now, because of his tattoo, he has engaged an opponent of a ferociousness he was unlikely to have foreseen. His inscription summoned forces never anticipated. With only minimal sense, his tattoo stimulated lethal rage. Merely through its attribute as a sign inscribed on his skin, it had a communicative power over and above the man's control.

When President Sukarno used the word rakyat he claimed to bring revolutionary forces into the nation. His assumption of the power of the people that animated him was akin to the communicative force of the tattooed criminal. The difference was that, via the people and the link they formed between family and nation, power was used to construct Indonesia, whereas with kriminalitas communicative force is not liberated and not constructive. There is, however, still reference to illegitimacy, as we shall see in the next chapter when we see how, in a rare instance, the figure of a criminal was constructed in the press.

Where does one look for criminal types? We look to journalism; there one finds not criminals in the sociological sense, but instead the manufacturing of images of criminals and ideas about their genesis. We start with *Pos Kota* (City Post). It is unique among Jakarta dailies not merely in appealing to the lower classes but in being a source of shame to middle class Indonesians who are caught with it in hand. It is unique too in its format, having as many as twenty photographs on its front page, most of them necessarily quite small, and often having fifteen or so stories that begin on that page. It concentrates on crime, but it also has pin-up photos, chaste by European standards, and stories about local politics and the difficulties of city life, featuring in particular traffic tie-ups and garbage collection.

Pos Kota is a New Order paper, that is, one belonging to the long epoch of Suharto. It was founded in 1970 by journalists who had been active in bringing down Sukarno.[1] It is a paper with a paternalistic ethos that the editors term idealism. The editors told me that in starting the paper they felt there was a need for a newspaper for "the lower classes" (*klas bawah*), no doubt because of the lack left by the closing of the leftist journals.[2] The paper was designed to be politically neutral, which, in the New Order, means progovernment or more exactly pro-Suharto. It does not feature much in the way of political news if that means stories of conflict. The people who run the paper feel a mission to enlighten the lower classes and to protect them. They therefore carry stories about inefficient services, such as the issuing of driving permits. Their attitude is reflected further in their statements about the language of the paper. Initially, they told me, the paper used the language of the street and featured short reports. But this was not welcomed by readers. The editors abandoned the language of the lower classes. In its place, they said, they gave their readers "lots and lots of details."

> If you talk to the people from the upper classes (*klas atas*) you only
> need two or three words. But if you speak to those below, you have to
> have details, lots and lots of details.

This description of the language of *Pos Kota* by an editor describes as well
the language employers use with servants or laborers and school teachers
with their pupils. It assumes the need for patience and a certain concern
not only for the understanding of those addressed but also for their
welfare.

One might think that such a voice goes oddly with contents that are
scandalous. It is impossible to say how readers hear the paper's tonality.
This reflects the more general problem of knowing in what capacities
readers of this paper read. And thus it is difficult to know what political
effects stories have. In any case, *Pos Kota*, though the firmest supporter of
the regime, claims it makes the censor nervous. He frequently phones with
"suggestions" even though, as I have said, overtly political stories—for
instance, of labor discontent or of corruption among the president's
family—do not appear. The problem is crime stories. The government
fears that too many of them will make people feel insecure, say the editors.
One can find quite ambiguous political messages in these stories, which
could also be why the censor calls quite often.

The same themes appear time and again: rape, incest, theft, and murder. But they are, without doubt, stereotyped. *Pos Kota* features a verbal
reconstruction of the crime as event. For instance, a story appears with
this headline:

> Asharudin Dead, Killed by his Own Nephew

The story begins:

> Asharudin, 41, stabbed by his own nephew in his house in Pasar Rebo
> Rt. 07/02, Jakarta Timur, Saturday night, finally died.

It continues to do what the editors say they do: give details that no doubt
add to the verisimilitude of the report. Characteristic of this sentence is the
contrast of this detail, which concerns the location, making the place
accessible to any reader who could simply go there, with the oddity of the
fact that Asharudin was stabbed "by his own nephew." Few readers are
likely to know who Asharudin was. But he is made known to readers as
much as he ever will be by the details contained in this sentence and the
next ones, where we learn that he was an employee of Djakarta Lloyd (but
what he did is not specified). He is part of a scene with which the reader is

expected to be able to be familiar not particularly because the reader knows already the types that work at Djakarta Lloyd or live at such an address but because he could go there. Instead of the paper furnishing more information, it puts the reader in the conditional mood: he could go there; he could meet if not the victim, his survivors and perhaps the criminal himself. Could is understood in this rhetoric even though the report seems to stick to the factual.

In *Pos Kota* Jakarta is a place of accessibility. It is always possible that one actually knows someone anywhere in the city or at least knows someone who knows someone and that one thus has access to anyone. Contained in this mental map is the assumption of social types. *Pos Kota*, in line with the government's policy of suppressing ethnic conflict, seldom identifies people by their origins. Jakartans, in any case, look for points of mutual acquaintance. If one is an army veteran who served under the same commander as someone else, for instance, one has such a point. Ethnic identification functions as another such element. Ethnic origin arises in conversation as one possible point that does not preclude others when it does not suffice. Jakarta, like much of the rest of Indonesia, thus is a place of potential recognition. This assumption is contradicted in *Pos Kota*'s stories in which, frequently, those one knows turn out to be unrecognizable.

Pos Kota's report of such incidents concentrates on the description of events.

> MK, with an unsheathed knife, after running amok, flagged down a passing Mikrolet passing in front of the house and asked to be taken to the nearest police station. At Police Station 705-01 Pasar Rebo, MK confessed straight away. He said he felt continually at odds with everything about his uncle. Another nephew, called Otong, was equally a victim. From the time he lived with his uncle [we did not know before this that he lived with his uncle] MK was put through school from grade school till he graduated from high school.

The report is told in the register of fact and as though information was simply gathered; it does not add up to an explanation. But one is not entirely expected. Rather, *Pos Kota* features the contrast between the possibility of such events occurring and being recorded and their sensational nature. It is once again the could that is implicitly understood; in the midst of the normal is the monstrous.

> From information gathered, the bloody event occurred at 7:00. Asharudin was watching TV at home. He had just returned from work.

Suddenly MK came out of his room and attacked his uncle. Without the chance to get out of the way, the victim, stabbed, bathed in blood, moaning from pain, called for help.

Pos Kota simply "gathers information" (as much from the police as from others). They only sometimes identify their sources. The report does not depend on witnesses' credibility. The facts are somehow facts in this newspaper without the need to question the reliability of those who claim to have seen the criminal act. This feature of their reporting, that the facts are not in doubt, doubles the assumption that whoever is arrested is guilty. One only occasionally hears of trials in the stories of *Pos Kota*. In this story, there was a confession. But even in the many others where no confession is noted, the assumption is the same: The person arrested is guilty. And the facts are as they are reported and as "information" has it.

There is, consequently, little questioning of motives. In this incident three sentences are devoted to a possible cause of the murder. They occur in the final paragraph:

> The victim left six small children. The family of the victim [but not who in particular] stated that they thought MK perpetrated his deed because he was out of work. His uncle had promised to look for work for him. But to the present he had not found any vacancies. MK kept demanding he look. The case now is being pursued by Police Post 705-01 Pasar Rebu. (4 May 1983)

There is a picture of perfect normalcy: A man with a large family who, in the manner of Indonesians, has also raised two nephews, returns home from work and watches television. A door opens and "suddenly" he is attacked and killed by a member of his own family. By someone who, it is implied, he would have every reason to trust, acting as he did as a father to his nephew. Between the crime and the normalcy intervenes a common social condition: unemployment, generating the nephew's resentment. The uncle, having done so much for the nephew, has taken the place of his father. From his father, his nephew/son expects more; it is the father's obligation. The failure of the obligation instigates the crime.

But nothing in the story blames the uncle. It is the reverse. The nephew is ungrateful; the uncle put him through school. In retrospect, at least, the family knew the nephew wanted his uncle to find him work; they imply that this is the reason for the crime. But this has the look of a retrospective view. We are given nothing of the circumstances, whether there had been disputes, why the nephew lived with his uncle, whether his uncle had tried to find work for MK. It is not a question of different points of view, of different claims that either side could make. And in any case, no matter how rooted the crime was in the obligations of kinship, such obligations tend toward the forbidding of this murder. The nephew should not have killed his uncle, in part because he was his uncle; and no one should have anticipated that he would do so. It is violence that was unexpected even if, afterwards, one could find a grievance. It is as much a monstrosity, an unnatural occurrence (the door flying open, the uncle surprised) as it is a conflict that arises out of social circumstances.

The crime here is a sort of fait divers, a curiosity. Nothing in *Pos Kota* leads one to suspect that one should be curious about anything other than the monstrosity, the unnatural, rather than the social generation of this murder. But this unnaturalness is smoothed away: The boy wanted his uncle to find him a job. The uncle did not; the nephew killed his own uncle. It is a syntax that in the end puts the ordinary and the institutional, the family in this incident, together with the unnatural and violent as what one can expect not to expect.

Some Stories of Kriminalitas

A policeman kills his superior.[3] It is not a familial crime this time, but it is treated in the same way. The superior had dressed him down in front of others. This is the reason for the crime. Once again it is both monstrous and natural. That is to say, the incident never creates doubt about the norms involved, about the conflict of identity between a police officer and a man with normal human feelings. Whether the superior behaved professionally, whether he should or should not have humiliated his subordinate in front of others and so on is not questioned. Of course it is not the role of the newspaper to put institutions in question. But, by giving so little of the intersubjective, one is left only with normalities and their contrary. And also, one is left with the criminal being only partially revealed. He remains the atypical example; the policeman who is a criminal, therefore a scandal, but, since untypical, easily forgettable.

One could cite other kinds of criminality, robbery for instance. One learns that robbers work in groups. But one never learns that these groups are bands, that they have their own areas of operation, their relations with other bands, their connections with the police, and so on. These structural questions are replaced by the repeated surprise that something untypical, a robbery, should happen in Indonesia. There is in these stories a reversal of the assumption of possible recognition that pertains in everyday life. In place of recognition, just where one thinks one knows already, one finds one does not know. Built as it is into the structure of the paper's narratives, one knows in advance what, as it were, not to expect.

It is in this monstrosity, this unnaturalness, that we first locate the kriminalitas of *Pos Kota*. It is simply what occurs, what disrupts, what goes without need for explanation but which occurs repeatedly and violently. As part of these assumptions, the criminal only partially comes into view. After all, what is a monstrosity if one can easily recognize it. MK is known only by his initials. If his photo appeared, it would have had a bar across his eyes. We would see that we can apprehend no more of his face than we can of his name from knowing only his initials. He appears only in order not to appear fully or to let it be known to readers that they cannot and perhaps need not know more than this. Indeed, *Pos Kota* is populated with criminals who are shown, it seems, in a code that, deciphered, lets the reader know he is not supposed to be able to recognize the criminal. The editors of *Pos Kota* claim they use initials and bars because of the law. But this cannot be the case as other journals do not do so. Rather, what one learns from looking at the front page of *Pos Kota*, even before one begins to read, is that there is something there that could be known, but this knowledge is prohibited.

Criminality, the general category that comprehends all specific sorts of crime in *Pos Kota*, would be the breaking of this general prohibition. Whoever is behind the mask, indicated by his initials, is a criminal. But the newspaper implys that it, too, would break the law if it let the criminal make himself known. Whether the reader would share in culpability or would be a further victim I cannot say at this point. But what is clear is the intent to claim a secret and in such a way that the reader knows there is one and knows that it is almost knowable. It is the strange feature of *Pos Kota* that criminals do not hide; they are hidden, and hidden in the name of the law. It puts the law breakers in the position of something waiting to be revealed. When one watches the readers of *Pos Kota* on the street as they abstractly stare at the paper, they give the impression of expecting something. Together with the criminals' photographs they seem two sides of an expectation.

Why should *Pos Kota* want to hide the criminal? Why do they, in the name of the law, but untruthfully, create a law of their own? They give a second reason. It is to save the families of the criminal from embarrassment. If the criminal were known, those who know him already, who know him most closely, would be ashamed. For *Pos Kota*, it is a question of the sort of paternal benevolence they claim as a principle of the paper. For instance, the editors cite the pay they give of their own accord, without contractual stipulation, to reporters who are ill, and the pains they take to see that the families of their employees are as well off as possible. They assume a position of benevolent surveillance and assistance. In the case of the partially identified criminal, they imagine a circuit of communication. There are those who would recognize the criminal's picture, even barred— the members of his family. There are others who would not but who, if his identity were revealed, would know him as the father or husband of some- one, perhaps their neighbor. It is similar to the assumption behind giving the address; anyone could go there and easily come to find, if not exactly to know, whoever lives at the address. Here, they have in mind preventing this. Precisely because it is possible to be found, it should be prevented. Not only embarrassment, but, one might suppose, possibly even further disruption is prevented when the criminal's identity is hidden.

The criminal initiates a circuit of communication between readers and those who appear in reports. The readers of *Pos Kota* figure from time to time in the news stories. Often, a reader will find in *Pos Kota* a description of an unidentified corpse, suspect it is a family member, find out that it is true, and have the story of their discovery reported in the paper (paying tribute, of course to *Pos Kota*). *Pos Kota* thus materializes as a player in the dramas of its readers. The criminal's name or his face could trigger other, more sinister, events. It is partly in the interest of keeping criminality a fait divers, a mere oddity, the unnatural, and not something of consequence. That identity is hidden just at the moment when the reader is enticed into wondering who the person is. It is not simply out of compassion for the family, but for the smooth operation of social life, for general social wel- fare. In doing so, *Pos Kota* creates a regulation. It comes not in response to the crime already committed, but happens in order to prevent further disruption and further possible criminality. *Pos Kota*'s law is designed to hinder acts and expression simply out of the feeling that something is there to be expressed and out of fear of the path that this expression would take. There are thus two vectors, opposed to each other, in the use of initials and barred photos. One tends toward revelation and the other toward discretion.

There are a few exceptions to *Pos Kota*'s rule of keeping the face of criminals disguised. One was named Kusni Kasdut. Kusni Kasdut's face and his name were published repeatedly. He was famous up through and after the moment of his execution in 1980. *Pos Kota* published a long series of articles about him in 1979 and 1980. His fame, or perhaps notoriety, rested on his ability to escape from prison and on his spectacular robbery of jewelry from the National Museum in 1963. He was convicted of killing a man he had kidnapped and he also killed a policeman who was trying to arrest him. He gave interviews to reporters from prison, probably in the interest of obtaining clemency after being sentenced to death. He told not simply stories of his crimes, however, but his biography. What he left is similar to the "autobiographies" of Sukarno and Suharto in that it is not written by the subject himself but by figures from the media. In Kusni's case there were two figures, there being two biographies, one of them based primarily on the series in *Pos Kota*.[4]

There are other similarities with Sukarno: the importance of the mother, poverty taken in other than a material sense, and ambiguity about parentage, a theme that once again is intertwined with the importance of the revolution. One of the repeated themes of Kusni Kasdut is that he is bewildered by the fact that the national police shot him when he had himself fought in the revolution. We will return to the place of his revolutionary participation in his crime.

In the account of his life Kusni Kasdut makes a distinction. There is the time when he lived with his mother and there is everything after that. This opposition includes the house where he lived, the place, Gang Jangkrik in the city of Malang, the poverty he endured, and his inability to successfully leave the house. It corresponds as well to a confessed inability to remember.

> The first 16 years of his life were a time of sleep (lelap) and remained obscure to him. From that span of time he could remember only where he lived, with whom and the atmosphere of poverty that enveloped him. Other than that, there was only darkness and sleep as though for his first 16 years he never existed. He does not like to discuss this. (Par, 22–23).

He knows that he was there, he existed, during the first sixteen years of his life, but he cannot remember any event, "as though for his first sixteen years he never existed." It is not that nothing happened. It is rather that it seems to him to have left no trace. At the same time, it bothers him. What would it mean to know that one had experiences that left no mark on one and, yet, which bothered one? And what if these were one's original experiences?

Kusni does not like to think about it and when he does, what he recalls—showing of course that there is memory—is that he did not speak. The paragraph continues:

> Because he was avoided by friends, he kept his mouth shut as much as possible. The result was that not a single friend was close to him. But if they had problems, he quickly involved himself, hoping to be able to exit from his tendency. But despite his exhausting efforts, the difficulty could not be overcome.

The phrasing is confusing. It seems as though his problem in speaking comes because he was avoided by his friends, and, because he spoke so little, his friends avoided him. When his friends are in need, and therefore, it is implied, more likely to listen to him, he speaks. But the tendency toward silence remains. What is clear is that during this period of darkness Kusni had no close friends and that is because of a difficulty of speech. Either he did not speak and did not have friends for that reason or he did speak and for that reason, he was avoided by friends and therefore refused to speak further. It is not that he could not speak; it is that his speech was ineffective or worse.

He finally attributes his difficulty with language and friendship to poverty. The next sentence:

> It was clearly because of the problem of money that those who surrounded him did not recognize him.

But he does not mention going hungry or lacking clothes, school fees, or, in fact, anything one might use money for. Lack of money results in lack of recognition that somehow renders Kusni's speech ineffective.

Poverty keeps him shut up with his mother and causes him shame. This is made clear in the *Pos Kota* account by S. Saiful Rahim, who later published one of the biographies of Kusni. Saiful Rahim's book opens with Kusni at the bus terminal where he goes during his youth to sell candy and cigarettes, not so much for the money as to escape the house.

> Kusni could not be a 'house cat' who did nothing but be fed. He felt pressured at home. Squeezed by a feeling whose origin he himself was unaware of. But he knew nonetheless that he felt it to be heavy and powerful. Even to the point where it ordered him to rebel. To oppose this constriction, this sensation of pressure. (SSR, 10)

One might think that this feeling of constraint and rebellion would be adduced later as the cause of his criminality. But it is not the case. The pressure of this account corresponds to the feeling in retrospect, described in the first book, of a past that leaves no trace, a time of darkness and unawareness where he knows that something happened but does not know exactly what. It establishes Kusni's youth as a time when he had to respond to something but was not sure just what it was, which later bothers him to the point where he does not want to discuss it but which, by the same token, is still present to him. This was associated with poverty.

Poverty, understood in Saiful Rahim's account, is lack of money, but it is just as much lack of others. This is, first of all, lack of anyone besides his mother, then nonrecognition by the world at large. The report continues where we left off:

> Perhaps because other than his mother he felt he had no one at all. He had no brothers or sisters or other relatives. He felt estranged and cast off by the wheel of fortune from the life of mankind in general. So it was that he felt continually pressured by his environment and called on to flee in a freedom which, in truth, also did not recognize him.

Here poverty means no relatives and almost no one else. He is left with his mother and feels "continually pressured." The nature of this pressure is further specified. If it seems to come from somewhere other than his mother, from his general surroundings, it is associated most strongly with his mother.

Kusni's mother, we are told, loved him dearly and provided for him. But this did not provoke the same response as that reported by Sukarno in the midst of the latter's poverty. What Kusni's mother gave him did not appear as a gift, making up for the lack of material wealth. Rather, her efforts for him made him feel how much he lacked:

> Each time he returned home to Gang Jangkrik, Kusni did not feel he was heading toward peace. He did not feel he was pointed toward a tranquil paradise filled with benevolence and protection for him. Rather he felt he was headed for hell, a place of implacable constriction. A hell filled with lashing pain and suffering. In fact he knew that at home he would meet his mother who loved him so very much. (SSR, 10)

It is tempting to stop here and conclude that his mother was his problem. That, in the cliché of popular psychology, he felt suffocated by his mother, a constriction that, indeed, would leave him closely comparable to Sukarno because, in this view, the constriction of the mother proceeds from the fact that she raises desire and yet is forbidden to offer full satisfaction. One might expect, for instance, a story of the rejection of women founded on the impulse to reject his mother. But in this account, there is a different turn. The pressure Kusni feels arises from his mother, but only because in his mother he sees that he has no father:

> He could not bear to see the weariness hidden behind the look and the smile of his mother. Even though his mother always smiled and always wore a look full of hope and gave him confidence in himself, Kusni, this well loved child could read what was hidden behind all this. He could read the extensive suffering behind his mother's smile and cheerful look. Therefore, each time he watched his mother make her way through the difficulties of life Kusni asked himself: Where are the others? Where is father? Where are the relatives? Where are the brothers and sisters? Where is mother's family? Where? Where? Wherrrrrrre? Where are they all? (SSR, 12)

Kusni Kasdut finds in his mother the opposite of the way she intends to present herself. She wants to give him courage or confidence in himself and to fill his needs. He, however, feels that she cannot give him enough. No matter how much she gives, she lacks something fundamental. She cannot be both his mother and his father. The result of this lack, we will see, is that he later finds phallic women whom he takes as lovers. He gains a certain masculinity, a masculine power, not from males, not from his father, but from women.

We will return to Kusni Kasdut's relation to women later. For the moment, let us return to his mother. Kusni's mother gives him everything a mother could give. But Kusni, "this well loved child" finds in his mother's giving, "only the weariness behind his mother's smile"; he finds only the inadequacy of her energy. As a result home is for him a "hell filled with lashing pain and suffering. In fact he knew that at home he would meet his mother who loved him so very much." Lacking a father, Kusni's mother cannot be a mother. Her love is only torment which, though at his origin, leaves no trace on him.

Kusni never mentions a debt owed to his mother in the manner of Sukarno speaking of his mother. He nevertheless feels her effects on him as precisely the lack of trace left by his youth. The lack he feels in remembering her is, of course, quite different than the nostalgia of someone like Sukarno who remembers what his mother gave him, thinks of her absence, recalls what he misses, and so on. Kusni knows or acknowledges his mother's sacrifices on his behalf, but this translates into her failure to give to him effectively. He cannot put this period aside; he feels obliged to tell reporters about it even though they do not make any explicit connections between this period and his criminality. They merely register what he tells them. They do so under the sign of poverty, the same poverty as Suharto's, felt as shame and with no connection drawn between that and later events. It is this poverty that Suharto's program of development (*pembanguan*) is designed to efface. It is there as something to be put out of memory, with no positive effects, not even the instigation to later accomplishments. And this, in turn, is linked to the lack of a father.

The more the mother gives, the more the son feels she cannot give him what he wants. It is a contradiction he cannot resolve. Not even later, when he becomes a successful thief. It is never said, for instance, that he stole in order to be wealthy and thus to make up for the poverty of his youth. The lack that originates with his relation to his mother persists. Its effect on him, he claims, or it is claimed by these reporters, is to isolate him from the world. His mother's inability to register on him is repeated in his inability to register with his friends. He is inarticulate, unable to speak for himself and with no one to speak for him, and he remains that way until the revolution.

Lack of a father makes him wonder if he is illegitimate.[5] This worry again leads him back to his mother. Only through her can he find out the truth of his parentage. She, however, decides not to tell him anything. Later, in what is taken as the fact of the matter, it turns out that Kusni's mother was married, had a daughter, and was left a widow. She lived with the older brother of her husband, a peasant called Wonorejo. Wonorejo had eight children when his wife died and he began a relation with Kusni's mother. They kept their connection a secret "at a time when social norms were strict" (SSR, 16). Then, when his mother was pregnant with Kusni, it could no longer be concealed; villagers were offended. Wonorejo married Kastum, Kusni's mother, in secret but villagers discovered the secret. The secret is double: They married after Kusni's mother was pregnant with him, and his parents were relatives who should not have married at all. Rahim makes clear that there was a scandal that he relates first in terms of the confusion of relationship: Kusni's sister, Kuntring, was also his aunt. That is, the marriage was considered a violation of the rules of permissible marriage and thus a form of incest. Rahim emphasizes this scandal:

> Kastum's presence as stepmother of eight children who were her nephews and nieces was not approved of by Wonorejo's relatives. Not only because a stepmother always has a bad image but because the situation of this particular stepmother was indeed different. Her presence [as stepmother] was not usual. Not only because she was pregnant before marriage, but also because she was *bulik* [aunt] of

eight orphans. By the norms of this village this event was not only unique and undesirable, it was also repugnant (aib). (SSR, 16)

This is the secret his mother kept from him. By implication it is presented in these accounts as the "pressure" Kusni felt, as though he knew it all the time without being fully conscious of it.

There are two elements in the discovery of Kusni's illegitimacy. First, the question of incest, it is implied, is there by the standards of the village. The further implication might be that such a marriage would be seen differently from the point of view of national standards. It seems thus to contradict our assertion that illegitimacy is feared after one becomes a nationalist. But this is not quite the case. The incest taboo might have been located in the customary and not the national sphere. But in the narrative as it is presented, Kusni fears being illegitimate before he knows about it. What makes him sense that he is illegitimate is his poverty, which he confounds with his lack of a father, hence illegitimacy. His conception of poverty is the same as Suharto's or Sukarno's. We have seen already that his poverty is not described as material. It is not an absolute, but a relative concept. It is relative to the ability to circulate in the wider, that is, national society. It is from this point of view, after the fact, that, through poverty Kusni fears illegitimacy.

Kusni learns about his father during the revolution. Hearing of the battle of Surabaya, he decides to join the revolutionary forces. Afraid that Malang too will be attacked and his mother forced to flee, he asks her where they might meet. She tells him she will go to their village. He is astounded. He never knew they had a village. He thought all the time that he and she too were born in Malang.

> "In Blitar!" gasped Kusni. The word felt strange to him. "In Blitar!" his mother repeated. "Your father was the village head man there."
>
> "Village headman!" Kusni gasped again. "If that's the case, we aren't so poor as I thought." There was a note of cynicism in his words. (Par, 57)

She then tells him that the woman who sometimes came to visit them was his older sister. He asks why she does not live with them. She once did; he does not remember. But her father asked to have her stay with him. Kusni's mother tells him that she left because his father took a second wife. He was six when they came to Malang. Then she tells him that his father is dead. He died during the occupation, trying to protect his people. All of this is lies and we are told that Kusni almost immediately suspects that is the case.

> But for no reason he knew of, the story could not lift the cloud over his heart. It felt as though something was left out. And reasonably enough. Why had his mother never told him this before? . . . And why did his father, the village headman's family never visit them? (58)

He feels there is something missing from the story. Why wouldn't she have told him it earlier?

> If only, if only, he could be certain he could be rid of this burden; the clouds would clear away and life would be clear. Obviously this story simply passed by, leaving no trace in him. (58)

If only he had been able to believe the story, his gloom would have dissipated. But the story "leaves no trace inside him." On the one hand, he cannot believe what his mother tells him. On the other, he is sure she knows something essential about him which he does not know himself.

> "I would be happier if you said that I am an illegitimate child, just so long as that is the way it was."

His mother, in this fictionalized version,

> could no longer hold back her tears which flowed down her cheeks. "Kus, Kus," his mother asked. "Do you think your mother would lie?"

Of course, his mother did lie. Kusni does not hold this against her according to both versions, but S. Saiful Rahim tells us that he was initially greatly disappointed in her. But she lied for his good to give him confidence in himself by giving him confidence in his origins. His conflicted attitude is shown by the description of his response:

> Kusni did not answer. But various thoughts swirled through him. What if it were true that he was an illegitimate child? Would it be better to hear his mother's confession than a fairy tale like that one?
> O, darkness. (58)

He goes himself to Blitar where he finds the first story was untrue. He confronts his mother with what he has learned; she tells him the truth.

The story of his father comes out only at a certain moment. It is the time when he, hearing of the battle of Surabaya, is about to go off to fight the British troops who are in the process of reestablishing colonial power. It is a moment when he fears that he could be definitively separated from his mother. This, of course, is what he is said to have desired. He would like to escape the house, the neighborhood.

The revolution gives him the acceptance he seeks. He finds a family who takes him in without asking about his origins and with whom his poverty makes no difference. This is a family of revolutionaries. It is in Surabaya, during the battle there. The family is composed mainly of youths, male and female, who feed him and give him a place to bathe and to rest. They banter, joke, exchange news of the battle and he is included:

> Kusni was filled with enthusiasm. What was this? Was it this that they called friendship? They did not do much. Just let him sleep and eat there and stare in the mirror. He did not do anything. Just look after the child and then just now and then; and lend them his weapon while he was there. All the same it was so warm, so direct, so intimate. There was Purnomo who was so wild. And Subagyo who was so casual. And the shy Rahayu. And the mother who was so supple. They were poor and probably there was no longer a father. Ah, why didn't he ask at the time? (Par, 76)

Thus during the revolution Kusni finds what he had wanted before. Those he meets during that period accept him and cause him no shame. They are poor like he is but poverty creates no barrier. There is no father in evidence, but this does not inhibit their sociability. Revolutionary society offers him a certain recognition, within the confines of the youth whom he knows and their families.

The revolution gave him the entry into the world that his lack of a father had deprived him of. When he hears about his own illegitimacy during the revolution it is no longer of the same importance. In the family that shelters him in Surabaya there is no father and it makes so little difference he forgets to ask where, exactly, the father is.

The revolution is also the occasion for him to make up for the lack of a father that he finds through his mother in another sense in the account of Parakitri.[6] At a certain moment Kunsi returns to Malang from Surabaya. Arriving there he comes across a formation of troops, male and female, with a banner announcing KRIS. The formation breaks up and Kusni looks on from a distance:

> A girl stood there, her arms on her hips. She wore a military uniform. A pistol in its holster slung from her waist. Her hands were soft and white with pointed fingers. Her hair was cut short, curled back on the sides and gathered in back.
>
>   What attracted Kusni to this woman was not her prettiness or the fullness of her body but something else. Kusni tried to think what it

was. Maybe it was her uniform and that pistol, so strange and daring when fused with a woman. (Par, 94)

This is the first of the phallic women Kusni falls in love with during the revolution, the next one being also a soldier, in fact, an *overste* (lt. colonial) who is later similarly described and whom Kusni loves for her uniform and her pistol. The first of these is also the first woman with whom Kusni makes love. She is from Menado and she teaches him Western-style dancing and other daring activities. She makes him feel he should not be angry with his mother for lying to him because she never asks about his father and because she is attracted to Kusni (Par, 96).

Kusni marries neither of these women. His wives are quite different and are described for their domestic qualities alone. These phallic women, however, Kusni loves because he sees maleness in them. This of course is not wholly different from the way Kusni saw his mother; each gift she gave him made him think of his missing father. But what he felt lacking in his mother he finds in Winnie, as this woman is named in the book.[7]

It does not last. After the revolution he marries someone quite different. And after the revolution what he wanted seems not less desirable but less legitimate. Then he is aware that the women he loved were communists and that his desire led him to disapproved of and, by later standards, dangerous liaisons. These were dangerous both morally and politically; these are ties that, had they been maintained, would have brought him into conflict with the state after 1965. These liaisons are, furthermore, connected, after the revolution, with his criminality. He brings the jewels he has stolen from the National Museum to a fence. The house of the fence is also a Gerwani headquarters, a headquarters of the Indonesian communist women's organization. It is while sitting in this house that he remembers his former loves because of their resemblance to the women there.

This incident is filled with ambiguities. There is the fact that he falls in love not with the women but with their pistols and their uniforms. In one register it means that he got what he lacked with his mother or, one can now say, what his mother lacked. In another register, one can say that he falls in love not with women but with the revolution; women only wear revolutionary attributes. It is the power of the revolution that substitutes for the missing male power of the absent father. Women are the means to obtaining this male power.

But if he has what he wants, it is only during the revolution, during the time that ordinary law is lifted and revolutionary law prevails. Later, by two standards, what he had then is seen to be ambiguous. By the standards of morality that prevailed before the revolution and which prevail again afterwards, the objects of his desire are not legitimate. And, by the political standards of the New Order Kusni was equally enamored of forbidden objects.

As he is pictured as remembering his affair with Winnie, he sees in retrospect that he did not understand what was happening either to him or around him. Winnie calls him a coward for at first refusing to learn Western-style dancing, then considered quite daring in Indonesia. She also teaches him how to kiss in Western style. But in the middle of their pleasure, Winne would "often come out with talk that was strange to Kusni." This talk is the communist line on revolutionary politics. Winnie derides Kusni's naiveté; he cannot understand what she says.

> It was true that he only fathomed a part of what Winnie said. Kusni indeed paid little attention to all the whispering and rumors that goes with that sort of politics. He just went his own way. (Par, 103)

The whisperings of love and the whispering of politics are mixed. Kusni understands only one part. But the fullest manifestation of his revolutionary feelings are with revolutionary communists. It is not communism that makes him a criminal to the degree to which he accepts the charge of naiveté. But it is mixing with these communist women that, being the most intense sentimental expression of his revolutionary identity, seems to implicate him nonetheless. He is like those classed as C after the round up of Communists with the change of regime. C was reserved for those who were influenced in one way or another by communists without being aware of what they were doing.

We are left with a picture of someone who, as a revolutionary, gains respect and even legitimacy, but who, after the revolution, as a revolutionary also, finds himself again guilty. Kusni wanted revolution. He found it; he enjoyed it; he loved it. And later he is guilty despite himself. Revolutionary fervor leads him, innocent of what he is doing, to communist women. The association between these women and revolutionary ardor is made explicit. It is not merely in the story of Kusni Kasdut that one finds the association between desiring women and revolution, of course. Stories of Gerwani debauchery were common from the early days of the massacre of communists. Such stories can also be found of the battle of nationalists and communists during the revolution.[8] The desire that the revolution tolerated and on which it depended is intolerable afterwards.

From the point of view of the New Order, communists should never have been allowed to play a role in the nation. They were deprived of the possibility after 1966. Kusni had a legitimate place in the nation only during the revolution. Before that, he was, as we have said, enclosed in the house. Afterwards he was a criminal. Kusni's criminality is not pictured as a version of communism. But it is parallel to it in that it, too, is seen as the continuation of violent power after the revolution ended. Communism here, as in other accounts, is conflated with desire. But doing away with communism does not do away with desire. Kriminalitas is the noncommunist form of this persistence in the story of Kusni Kasdut.

After the revolution Kusni does much of what he did during it. Now, however, these acts make him a criminal. During the revolution Kusni led a band that robbed Chinese and gave the proceeds to those active in the revolution. Kusni, we are told, did not know and did not want to know what happened to the proceeds. He furnished "tens of millions" for the revolution. "If in this way he had made a difference to those who wanted freedom, he was satisfied" (Par, 139). Later, after the revolution, he is shot as he tries to escape from prison. He is pictured reflecting on the robbery he committed from the National Museum:

> What was the difference between the diamond from Gorang-gareng and the one from the museum? What was the difference stealing from a family, from someone from one's own nation who lived in Gorang-gareng and stealing from the museum in Jakarta, the property of the Indonesian nation? There was no difference! A diamond is a diamond. Stealing is stealing.
> But there was a great difference!
> Stealing the diamond in Jakarta he went to Mlaten (the locale of a prison). Stealing the diamond in Madiun, he went to Jogjakarta, the capital of the republic. In Mlaten he was put in a cell. In Lempuyangan, Jogjakarta, he was put into a room in the Pandu Teratai barracks. (Par, 164)

"A diamond is a diamond. Stealing is stealing." The only difference is what the nation makes of it. During the revolution, theft means acceptance by the Indonesian national forces. Afterwards it means being cast out of national life. The activity is the same; the difference is whether there is revolution or not, whether revolutionary legality applies. The criminality of Kusni is an effect of acting like a revolutionary after the revolution. In that sense, one can say that it is the revolution itself that makes Kusni a criminal. It is the continuation of his revolutionary activity after the time of the revolution.

During the revolution, the Chinese whom Kusni robbed had no right to their property. The revolution needed funds and they were obliged to help. Taking from them, in that sense, was not considered theft. The sense of this paragraph is that in a period where private property has a very low claim, Kusni not only has a right to do what he did, but doing it made him heroic.[9] He furnished "tens of millions" for the revolution. His activity singled him out. He had an exceptional power.

Indeed, as we have said, Kusni Kasdut was reported to have supernatural power that he exercised particularly in escaping from prison. Kusni Kasdut was criminal because he held on to a fetishistic power after the period when his fetishism was legitimate. But Sukarno, the extension of the tongue of the people, was no less fetishistic after what he called the "physical revolution" ended. Sukarno's fetishistic power, by contrast, precisely claimed to generate recognition. It is the point of the speech we quoted in the last chapter and numerous others. Sukarno, speaking for the masses, made them into the people; his "revolutionary economics" made their poverty into symbolic richness, an expression of Indonesia's unique traditions as subject to revolutionary thinking. His transformation of revolutionary fervor into nation building took account of familial origins.

Kusni's power never articulated his origins with the nation except during the revolution and then only negatively. Kusni found in phallic revolutionary women what his mother could not give him. But this was mere displacement. It never resulted in the conjunctions of Sukarno through which he remembered his mother and served the people at the same time. In the accounts he remained a figure of a force that could not be controlled. He was executed, but the continuation of kriminalitas shows the fear that this force was not extinguished.

Disarticulation

When one looks at questions of legitimacy there are two steps in the story of Kusni Kasdut. There is the question of illegitimacy and its relation to nationalism and revolution. Similar to the presidents of his nation, the story of Kusni traces a path out of the family and turned questions of illegitimacy into legitimacy and recognition gained during the revolution. There are, in these stories, the question, often raised in the biographies of men of the period, of the failure of fathers with recompense for that failure gained in nationalist struggle. But in the stories of the presidents, revolutionary activities lead to a place in the nation. For them, there is no difference between nationalism and revolution. But with Kusni this is not the case. He continues to act as he did as a revolutionary after the winning of independence. This, according to Parakitri, is linked to his association with phallic communist women. He gains a power through them that is never domesticated, that is never brought into the service of the nation after independence and, in fact, is confounded with his criminality. Kusni was not a communist, but he demonstrates that containing desire in "proper" channels after revolution was not achieved with the suppression of communists. His kriminalitas is the continued expression of desire without a "normal" mode of expression. In the end, revolution makes up for the failed father, is the source of male power, and, for a while, of legitimacy. But as the nation reinstitutes familialism Kusni rests as an example of the continuation of the revolution and hence as the disguised source of kriminalitas.

Kusni Kadut is a construction of journalism. He is an exception, as I have said, in that he is a well known criminal, celebrated by the media. He is treated in three different ways. One, which I have not emphasized, is the picture of him as a husband and father. He tells his son not to take him as an example. His wife is pictured as knowing nothing of his criminal activities, merely treating him as a normal husband. She tells reporters, for instance, what food he liked and did not like. The major difficulty of the stories of Kusni is knowing whether to consider him a traditional bandit, a revolutionary, or a contemporary figure, a father and husband like others, but one gone wrong.

One can compare him briefly with the traditional Javanese *jago,* which can be translated as bandit only with much modification. The jago was a thief and murderer used by the lower levels of colonial administration but also hunted down by them. He had a place within the system of administration without, however, being legitimate. At the turn of the century he was celebrated in stories and reports, but only ambiguously. Henk Schulte-Nordhoff shrewdly says that he was the subject of "entertainment," thus contained within the faits divers of the day.

Kusni Kasdut has elements of the jago. He is an exception, as I have said, in that his feats, particularly his escapes from jail, were celebrated and were attributed to his magical powers, again in the manner of jago. When one compares the production of films and books in the Philippines that feature bandits, one sees how Indonesia is different. Jago and criminals furnished much of the push for revolution. But they had never been part of the national celebration of revolutionary heros on any scale. The failure to make them so is part of the suppression of the revolution in favor of a domesticated nationalism to which I have already referred. But they are held in reserve in the faits divers. Occasionally one such as Kusni Kasdut emerges. In him we see how his revolutionary past remains ambiguous. It is, no doubt, precisely this ambiguity that makes it difficult to generate heroic narratives. It is, rather, his quality as a jago, thus out of place in the modern nation, that is celebrated while at the same time he is pictured as a pathetic example of someone who is either a strayed contemporary figure or, in place of showing him as a revolutionary who remains such and is out of place, a revolutionary gone astray.[10]

Kusni Kasdut was already present in the Sukarno period and to that degree he shows that Sukarno's use of the word rakyat was inadequate. He is not thought of as betraying the revolution; he is, rather, seen as the revolutionary going astray. It is not his bid for power but the inability of Indonesian leadership to harness it that one sees in the accounts of him. It is the fear that such revolutionary power still exists and that it remains without articulation. Without articulation in the sense that Sukarno spoke for the people only inadequately and Suharto not at all. The masked criminals of Pos Kota, striving to reveal themselves, show the Indonesian world that a disruptive force is still pushing for expression. Kusni in the Sukarno period was merely a revolutionary turned robber. In the Suharto era he was one of thousands, a manifestation of something generic, kriminalitas, that arose as the possibility of articulating the revolution lessened.

As we have described him, Kusni Kasdut, and kriminalitas as well, arises in the place of the word rakyat. Pronounced by Sukarno before the masses, rakyat brought these masses into the nation. Left practically unspoken by Suharto, these masses are left out. But what exactly does it mean to be left out? And can a word with such potency and such an important place in political rhetoric be simply put aside? Can one determine that it be forgotten? Can it simply cease to function?

The first word to stand in the place of rakyat as a performative was PKI. This is the abbreviation for Communist Party of Indonesia, but it was used in the 1960s to designate not the party but its members, as in "he is PKI." In 1965 and later this phrase amounted to a death sentence. It is as such that it is comparable, though by no means identical, to rakyat. Sukarno's enunciation of rakyat brought it into being, making of the persons hearing him its constituent parts. By contrast, PKI was a name that was followed by the extinction of its referents. In that sense, this word "disarticulated," separating as it did the name from the living person. In view of the elimination of the communist contribution to Indonesian history it is also anti-figural, aiming at the elimination not only of the referent but of its memory, the figures that might endure despite the death of persons. When PKI is mentioned today it evokes an amorphous demon rather than a determined figure. PKI lacks the stereotypes of racism or antisemitism. It is not the form, the shape, the image in the strong sense of that term, or the metaphorical representation that the term designates. It is the separation of its elements that leaves one of them absent, the effect of disarticulation.

But PKI is not a verbal memorial, the survival of the name after the death of the person. There is still a force in the word. It is one that presses even though it no longer articulates; it does not bring the Communist party or its utterances back on the scene. This force emerges again in the name Kusni Kasdut, which expresses the continuation of the same force after communists disappeared from the Indonesian political scene. It is the continuation of a sensation of menace.

Turn back for a moment to Asharudin. In his case we saw the failure of the familial idiom; the uncle/father who, in the eyes of his nephew/son, failed to give as expected. The nephew/son murdered Asharudin because the latter was not the uncle/father the former expected him to be. This failure came precisely at the point of juncture of the family and the wider society when Asharudin did not find work for his nephew. His nephew then no longer saw in him an uncle. And Asharudin, when his nephew came through the door at him, knife in hand, must not have recognized his nephew any longer as his nephew. No nephew he had done so much for would do such a thing to him.

Who, then, was it who killed Asharudin? It was someone for whom the transition between family and nation had failed to take place. Someone like Kusni Kasdut, isolated in the family and lacking a way out. Were the nephew's insistence to have had a positive outcome, it would have resulted in the uncle finding work for him; hence in his translation outside the family. As it stands, the murder exposes a rage for exit from the family that no longer can be attached to the person of the nephew. MK, his initials, indicate merely a force wanting articulation. Hence the failure not only of the family but of the nation, which in the New Order provides the nephew with no substitute for his uncle. What is left is an explosive energy, located inside the family, always available for expression, forcing its way out with no definite end in sight. It is hard to distinguish from revolution.

Words of disarticulation fill in the place left vacant by rakyat and "revolution," aiming to reverse the effects of that word. But the force that generated rakyat continues. It is against the possibility of it regenerating forms of expression that terms such as PKI and Kusni Kasdut, which first indicated figures, become words of disarticulation. This development is of course always too late.[11]

3 In Lieu of "The People":
The Replacement of Ghosts

Only one kind of lie has a chance of being effective: that which in no way deserves to be called deceit, but is the product of a lively imagination which has not yet entered wholly into the realm of the actual and acquired those tangible signs by which alone it can be appraised at its proper worth.
—*Thomas Mann*, Felix Krull, Confidence Man

The Palsu

The Indonesian press, both the lower class papers such as *Pos Kota* and the middle class journals, frequently have stories of the *palsu*, the counterfeit. These are usually stories of fraud or theft, but not always. Many things can be counterfeit: trademarks, bills, deeds, divorce certificates, bus tickets, court documents, whiskers on a robber used for disguise, holdups (to conceal embezzlement), license plates, *dukun palsu* ("false magical curers" or "those who only pose as curers"), permits to make the pilgrimage to Mecca, revenue stamps, and pirated music tapes. The list is by no means exhaustive. There is an entirely fictive university, granting degrees to those who then teach in other universities. The head of this university (which consists of only the rector and the dean), explained:

> They want to be university graduates but they have never been able to do so, said the father of 6 children to Taufik Abriansjah from *Tempo*. So, we made Unidu [an acronym for Universitas Dipati Ukur] out of a technical high school. Here degree candidates don't have to spend a lot of time going to class. With Rp1.5 to Rp3 million—depending on the final certificate of the candidate—Unidu can quickly confer a certificate of "sarjana" [more or less the equivalent of BA]. ("Universitas Bodong Bung Tohang," *Tempo*, 28 November 1996: 93)

The university has no campus, no teachers, no classrooms, and no students, much less a curriculum. Some of their graduates now teach at Ar-
Rahmaiyahr University in Bogor. The rector of that university is the rector
of Unidu, and the dean of Unidu is a teacher there. Jailani, the rector, says
that Unidu graduates were given their *sarjana* degree "only for internal
use" at the other university. He thinks it is not illegal. It is like the open
university; it works by mail. He seems to be unashamed; merely perform-
ing a service for those who want it. What he evokes as its legality is
demand. People want a degree; he sells them one.

The university's lack of content seems not to bother him. He says that
none of his graduates feel they have been harmed. And he warns them not
to use their degrees to look for a job. The police chief disagrees; it is
not only society (*masyarakat*) but also the nation (*negara*) that can be
harmed. What happens when Unidu graduates become civil servants
(*pegawai negri*)? The minister of education and culture, Fuad Hasan, is
upset. The government tries to raise the caliber of education and then
there is this.

One notes how fraud spreads. Unidu is clearly palsu. But Ar-Rahmai-
yahr University is ambiguous. It lacks government certification, but the
lack of training of its faculty is not apparent. It makes one imagine Ar-
Rahmaiyahr University, which actually holds classes for its students, send-
ing its graduates to teach in government certified universities. Eventually
the difference between true and false universities would be unclear. There
would remain, perhaps, governmental certification, but given the numerous counterfeit government certificates, one could not be sure even of
this, even if one wanted to accept governmental certification as proof of
the quality of university education.

It is a familiar situation of early capitalism and it effects business most
of all. One might think that the problem is that everything, including
education, including magic, becomes business; but this is not entirely
accurate. In any case, it is business that is most effected. Take a report from
Pos Kota concerning Bata shoes. A store near the port of Jakarta sells Bata
shoes marked with the code "E." The police seize the shoes but they are
sure that there are many more still for sale in Jakarta and in other cities.
These are palsu and there is material loss. Buyers are disappointed to find
that their children wear their new shoes, walk through a few puddles and
the soles come loose. As a result, buyers are "on the look-out against the
palsu," says *Pos Kota*. The paper explains the complications of this falsification. Buyers complain; there is an investigation that uncovers "a clever

arrangement between insiders (orang dalam) and suppliers which, directly or not, aids those who dilute Bata production."

AF, San, and his boss worked for Bata shoes. They bought from various suppliers, including one with the initials TNK who was arrested, who manufactured shoes with various codes: N, G, K, and P. Through DD, these shoes were redistributed to retailers. The retailers marked them up 40 percent, whereas they ordinarily got only a 5 percent markup while AF, San, and DD also profited. It is not clear which stores were aware that they were getting cheaply made shoes with the Bata trademark.

What is remarkable, but common in stories of falsification, is that the source is no guarantee of authenticity. The Bata trademark was not counterfeit; it was genuine. But through these insiders cheap shoes replaced higher quality goods. This is a version of the counterfeit so common that there is a neologism, *aspal,* stemming from an acronym, to designate it. Aspal is derived from *asli* or original and palsu. The word was used, for instance, to describe the use of genuine certificates asserting that the person named is a veteran, hence eligible for a pension. The person named on the certificate was already deceased. It is a feature of this sort of counterfeit that there are "insiders" involved who furnish the genuine-but-false verification or mark; it might be, as in certain cases, government certificates. In one instance, a man who worked as a guard at the entrance to an Office of Religious Affairs arranged with people he knew who worked there to pass some divorce certificates on to him. Familiar with the ways of the office, he filled them out and sold them to those in need. He was only caught when a pregnant woman was handed a certificate of divorce by her husband who wanted to take a second wife. His first wife objected. He was a civil servant and needed his wife's consent to marry a second time. She complained and the certificate was discovered to be false. That is, it was real-but-false.

In this case, the counterfeiter, if one can properly call him that, made some mistakes. He began to print his own forms, copying those of the Religious Affairs Office. He also signed them. Here he was careless but, as he told the reporter, "It didn't matter; people don't pay much attention to the signature." No one detected the invalid signature until after the wife complained. He made other mistakes as well. The genuine forms come in three colors, one each for the husband, the wife, and the office. His came only in black and white, not because he did not know, but because few are familiar with the forms.

Tempo, the middle class news magazine, is careful to mention these mistakes, probably for the same reason *Pos Kota* mentions the code on the true-but-false Bata shoes: consumers can look out for the falsification. But this knowledge is not likely to be practical in the case of the divorce certificates that circulated only in a small town on a remote island. It is rather that these reports rely on an interest of Indonesian readers that contrasts with the interest in clues of readers of Western detective fiction. In the latter cases, one sees that one can know something from a small bit of evidence. The world consists of signs that are open to interpretation. The detective uses clues to uncover guilt. Neither in the Indonesian detective fiction I am familiar with nor in the newspaper do the police do anything similar. Falsity simply pervades the Indonesian world. One knows that one cannot rely on signs; they are as likely to mislead as not. In the case of the divorce certificates, for instance, it was not the discovery that the signs were false that led to the arrest of the counterfeiter. It was the woman's complaint. After that, it was discovered that the certificate was false. The same is true of Bata shoes. Only after complaints and the arrest of the culprits is it made known that the true-false Bata shoes are marked E, N, G, K, and P. The narrative model here is not the detective story but the ghost story, one familiar version of which is that one speaks with someone and later learns it was a ghost. But nothing at the time warned one. Looking back, if one had known that there was often a ghost at that location and known what he or she looked like, one might have known. But it is too late.

The interest of the writers of these stories is in the construction of the scheme. *Pos Kota*, we have seen, goes into much detail to describe the arrangements of retailers, manufacturers, and the Bata company employees. One learns how it was done.

> Seeing that people who wanted to be divorced only needed a sheet of paper as a certificate, he had an idea: to make false certificates.

After the complaint, investigators "seize as evidence a number of blank certificates." *Tempo*, like *Pos Kota*, tells its readers exactly how he went about it. Once having the idea

> With Rp30,000 in capital he had 500 forms printed and had a stamp 'UA Metro' [Metro Religious Affairs] made by someone on the street.

The interest, which amounts to concealed admiration, is for the schema; how it was done, how they went about it, is given in enough detail so that a scene is implied. One can imagine the directions the manufacturer of certificates of divorce gave to the man who made the stamp used on the form, for instance. By contrast, one does not see the work of the detectives who arrested him. Often it is simply the tools that attract attention. For instance in the case of a bank that held false deeds as collateral for loans, *Pos Kota* describes in some detail the way the forgeries were made and the instruments used:

> As described by [a police agent], the forgery was done by directly tracing, letter by letter, from a photocopy of a genuine certificate. The heading was done by typewriter. For the signature they did the same but they used a pencil and then made it stand out using a fountain pen. They had various fountain pens at hand for forging signatures.
>
> In the same way, they made the map of the plot, but they used a needle . . . they made 39 official seals which of course were also false. Among them were the seals of the Sub Direktorat Agaria East Jakarta, Tangerang, notary, Bureau of Registration and Verification of Deeds, Kelurahan and many other officials as well. ("Deeds and other certificates of ownership, *Pos Kota,* 29 November 1983)

In this description the character of the forgers is submerged in the action of their tools. Pencils, typewriters, needles, and pens work without mention of the agents that guide them. One sees one sheet of paper laid over another, the heading appearing as the effect of the action of the typewriter, the fountain pens laying ready for use, and so on, but nothing even of the identity of the technicians.

A short report of forged high school diplomas repeats this style of narration:

> It is thought that there are many forged diplomas still in circulation. The diploma forged is from the SMA (Senior High School) Arena Siswa II, Central Jakarta. The diploma was forged using an official stamp and a *palsu* signature of the Principal of SMA Arena Siswa II. ("Police Stop Diploma Forgery," *Pos Kota,* 8 September 1983)

It is not the illicit nature of this activity that is stressed; it is, again, the manufacturing of something: a scheme, a form, and so on.

The newsmagazine *Tempo* differs from *Pos Kota* in an important respect. *Pos Kota* describes the scheme and, in cases of counterfeiting, also the tools used. But it seldom tells its readers just how the idea occurred to the criminal. *Tempo* reports, for instance, that the man who counterfeited divorce certificates worked in a menial position at the Religious Affairs Office. There he helped the clients of that office. Anyone familiar with Indonesian bureaucratic offices will recognize the type. He has a position of little importance but he is useful as an intermediary. One can ask someone of his sort for help; he knows where one's papers are located, who to ask to attend to the matter, and so on. *Tempo* reports him saying, "In arranging a divorce there are a lot of hidden payments." Realizing this, he goes into business for himself. He, like the rector, is an amateur bureaucrat, doing what government bureaucrats do, only more; he helps people at the same time.

One cannot understand the lack of the sinister in these descriptions without seeing the admiration for doing something, for making something more efficiently if not always with a value that lasts, and without understanding that in some cases such people, in real life, actually do help one get, say, a driver's license in a few days rather than weeks or months. These people may cheat, but the esteem for them, even the recipes for being like them given by the details, is not explicable as a desire for transgression. The admiration is not for getting away with it, for defying authority. It is for creating a sort of authority for oneself. One has one's own rubber stamp. It explains the lack of rancor.

And the admiration for these fictions makes understandable the lack of charges of fake or hypocritical (*munafik*) that circulated under Sukarno. Hypocrisy is concerned with the difference between origin and expression. That is not exactly the interest in the palsu, a word taken not from Indonesian but from the English false, whose sense as it is used seems to me to be as much "almost valid" as "counterfeit." In the Indonesian press, what works is valid. It is why the rector of Unidu thinks he has done nothing wrong, rather the contrary. People want university degrees and it is acceptability that matters. The swirl of false documents, false shoes, counterfeit monies, is not necessarily outrageous; it rather testifies to the creative abilities of the counterfeiters.

In many of these reports one senses the increasing scale of these crimes; gangs become larger and involve insiders. But on the other hand there is the case we have just mentioned; a single man, quite poor, who simply goes into business for himself. *Pos Kota* also describes such people:

> Results of a Police Raid: A Family Prints Counterfeit Money Because They Want to Get Rich Quick (*Pos Kota*, 26 October 1983)

A family prints its own money. The police seize a decal-making machine, several sheets of paper, a paper cutter, and some chemicals. Those arrested were a man and his wife, the wife's father, and two accomplices. The crime was uncovered when someone tried to pass a bill and was refused. He remembered that he had changed it for a larger bill at a small stand. This stand or *warung* was run by the counterfeiters. The police went there directly and arrested them. They confessed to printing six bills of Rp1000 and two of 5000.

> The reason they dared to make palsu money, according to them, is that it is difficult to find work and they wanted to get rich quick.

Here is a crime, counterfeiting money, which one expects to take place on some scale. Yet it is a family operation. The family is poor; they run a street-side stand. They are naive enough to pass the bills to their customers. They do not think about being traced. And they do not seem to think a great deal about the vast wealth open to them if they were to increase their production of money, though of course, it would be nice. They remain who they were, poor people looking for work, not even desperate so far as one can see, who think that admitting to printing a mere eight bills is believable. And yet it is as if one assumes them to be, as many of the criminals of *Pos Kota* are said to be, readers of *Pos Kota*. One has only to get the necessary equipment and go into business for oneself. This is amateurism in all its senses. One makes money here the way I play the piano after hearing Rubenstein. They want to get rich the way I want to sound like him, with the same limitations of reality put out of mind. No matter how much the results fall short there is still a certain satisfaction.

They have the tools the way I had a piano. The opportunity arises in their minds because the possibility exists. The difference, among other things, is a difference of societies. I live in a society where being a counterfeiter is a possibility that exists enclosed by the strongest sanctions. But Indonesia in the New Order, as pictured in its press is a place of possibilities open to entrepreneurs at every social level and stimulated by the means at hand. Sanctions certainly exist and, so far as I know, in practice may usually operate effectively. But stories of kriminalitas in *Pos Kota* or *Tempo* are not so much concerned with transgression as with opportunity; and opportunity is seen in terms of the means of production.

Tempo reports the case of a man who multiplies money (*Tempo*, 6 August 1983: 59). The title, "Multiplying Money: Islamic Religious Leader from the Temple" refers to his house, a veritable palace, in Pamekasan Madura. Though the term is not used in the report, the man might be considered a dukun palsu, a false magician. Like other dukun, people come to him for winning lottery numbers. He gives them pieces of paper written on in Arabic script to use as charms. His falsity is seen by the charge of one man that he got such a charm with only the first half of the confession of faith (there is no God/[But God, Allah is his name]). The man thus accused this magician of spreading apostasy. His great crime is to make people believe they can multiply money. Someone gives him a bill. Standing in front of the giver, he produces two bills of the same denomination. They return with millions of rupiah. He keeps the money but he gives them a slip of paper with instructions to recite certain Koranic phrases on certain dates; then their money will multiply. It does not work. They return. He tells them another date; it still does not work. Certain of them come back to his house on the island of Madura and stay for as long as a year, reciting these phrases in ideal conditions. Finally they go to the police.

What attracts this man's victims is his demonstration of his ability. He makes their money double in front of their eyes. They want to do the same. Their mistake is to posit a mysterious power behind his drawing room trick. But it is not their mistake that interests us; it is their logic. This man has access to a certain power. They can use the same power once they know how. One has to have the tools, as it were. It is no different than the counterfeiters of money and other objects. They draw on the power of reference of the marks they imitate. They know these marks have a power inherent in them. One has only to be able to make the same marks, the same forms, the same signature and a couple is divorced, or a man can buy what he needs or people will give money for the mark itself when it is attached to a pair of shoes.

The cases of false curers (dukun palsu) are not different, structurally speaking, from other types of palsu. All the more so since there is no attempt to discredit the supernatural. Dukun palsu are, so far as I could find out, a phenomenon of the New Order. They exist as part of the interest in the palsu, which seems to invade nearly every part of daily life. There are, no doubt, several reasons that there is no move toward demystification. One of them surely is the interest in validity as what works rather than as original. The man who multiplies money by magic only has a different technique than the man who multiplies it by counterfeiting, or, for that matter, the Indonesian mint that prints bills legally. What is true of them all is an attraction to or a reliance on a notion of power behind the techniques. The dukun palsu may or may not think he is palsu; the issue never comes up. He becomes palsu when it becomes clear that he has not performed the way he should (and might) have.

I could not find the dukun palsu in the literature describing the pre-Suharto period, though there were always ineffective dukun and magical swindlers. The difference is that the palsu makes an implicit reference to its opposite, the authentic. Of course this authenticity is not located in the official. Not only is there no Bureau of Magical Curers to authenticate their skills, but, between the Indonesian mint and the counterfeiter on the corner, the difference, it is implied in these reports, is not the origin of the money but whether it circulates without difficulty. Of course, every counterfeiter in *Pos Kota* was caught. But the interest in the counterfeiter is less in making the contrast with the legal than it is in implying that there exists a power to make counterfeit money, or shoes, effectuate divorce, and so on, which is equally accessible to anyone with the right tools no matter whether they are official or not.

It raises the question of the role of the state. Take this story from *Tempo*, for instance, concerning someone *Tempo* labels a "false paranormal." ("Ulah Paranormal Palsu: Seorang karyawan perusahan swasta disiksa hingga mata kirinya buta. Polici terkecoh paranormal palsu?" *Tempo*, 5 December 1992) A man was beaten by the police, given electric shocks, whipped, forced to drink his own urine, and held under water. This was to force him to confess to a crime. It is not that the police tried to frame him, we are told. They were convinced of his guilt, not on the basis of ordinary evidence but because a "paranormal," the English term is used, told the police he was guilty. The victim claimed that someone in his office sent the paranormal to the police with the accusation in order to avert suspicion from himself for the crime involved. The mistake of the police in this instance is to have relied on a false paranormal. They paid no attention to the protest of the accused, who knew of the role of the paranormal. A genuine paranormal might have told the police who really committed the crime. Had the accused simply confessed it is unlikely that *Tempo* would have considered the role of the paranormal worth attention.

There is no demystification here. If anything, the idea of the false reinforces the idea of a power to be had by those with access to the techniques. The state does not claim to be the site of rationality guarding its citizens against the irrational. On the contrary, here the state relies on this irrationality. The assumption is that it cannot only use but magnify this power. The state thus puts itself in a position of possible rivalry with its citizens for control of this force. The printing of money, for instance, is not thought of differently.

There are two elements in the theme of the palsu. Common to other manifestations of kriminalitas, there is the idea that anything might occur. The palsu, indicating a true force, allows the possibility that anyone can govern an occurrence. The question becomes how. *Tempo* differs from *Pos Kota* in showing how interest is aroused. *Pos Kota*, for instance, speaking of counterfeiters, lists their tools as though the idea of tools alone is enough for someone to be interested in making their own money. They sometimes report the statements of the criminals: "There was no work," but they do not do as *Tempo* does, try to reconstruct the mentality of the criminal, as, for instance, when it reports the maker of divorce certificates first seeing the bribes paid and then saying, "he had an idea." *Tempo* gives its readers people with whom to identify themselves; *Pos Kota* gives them mainly tools and schema.

Tempo's stories picture an intersubjective world; there is the accused, the police, sometimes the accuser, and the victim, all of whom can speak to each other and to themselves as well as to the reporter. As a result *Tempo* makes guilt unclear; it even seems to make the question mark its preferred form of punctuation for its titles:

> A Fictive Deposit? The holder of Rp350 million at Bukopin cannot retrieve his money though the deposit has matured. Bukopin suspect the deposit is fictive. (*Tempo*, 26 December 1992: 84–85)

The question mark serves not only to raise doubt about the facts but to lead to further questions. The report begins by asking, "Are deposits in private national banks safe?" In this case, the possible crime occurred at the same time as one of Indonesia's major banks failed. *Tempo* did not hesitate to raise a fear for áll deposits in such banks. It is a feature of *Tempo*'s reporting that one question leads to another in such a way that a particular crime is made into a type and a national problem.

Djunkenadi Osadi is one of the biggest clients of the bank. He put 150 million into the bank in a three-month certificate of deposit. But he could not get the money back. First the bank said it was because of a difficulty with the new computer system; there was a virus. When the claim was put to the bank's office in Bandung, they also refused to pay, saying that the deposit was *fiktif*. The head of the bank where Djunkenadi Osadi had made the deposit, Budiman Witarsa, was fired because he was suspected of profiting from Rp.800 million in fictive deposits, using fifty Bukopin deposit slips. A fictive deposit, it is explained, is one not entered on the books of the bank. If the head of the bank is correct, no deposit was ever made. But the money was claimed on the basis of the (real-but-false) deposit slip. The case is further complicated because Djunkenadi had used the deposit slip as collateral for a loan at another bank. When this bank heard about the accusation of a fictive deposit, they blocked his transactions at their bank. Djunkenadi Osadi sued Bukopin for the money plus damages, which is how the case came to light. Once again a forgery, if it was that, was not known by the document itself; only after the fact was the document said to be false.

The facts in this case were further complicated because the bank had recently fired one of its employees who had used the fictive deposit schema to relieve Bukopin of millions of rupiah. "It's possible this is a product [*produk*] of a syndicate [*sindikat*] of robbers headed by Budiman Witarsa [the fired bank employee]," said the head of the bank. "[Djunkanedi] Osadi clearly is among those suspected," he added, a charge which Djunkanedi denied. At the time of the report, the last I could find on the subject in *Tempo,* the bank was willing to settle out of court.[1]

What is evident to *Tempo* is that somewhere there is something fiktiv. The question is what it is. It could be the deposit slip which, again, was real-but-false. It may have been printed by the bank, but no money was ever deposited. In this case there is the implication, made by the bank head, of an "insider," *Tempo*'s term, involved, someone who might, for instance, have arranged to have the filled-in deposit slip stamped by the bank without the deposit being made. The other possibility again implies an insider; the deposit was made but it was never entered on the books of the bank, someone retained the money. Or the bank might have entered the deposit and simply refused to return the money.

The bank first admitted that the deposit might not have been entered when it claimed a computer error. If this were the case it would mean that the deposit was never registered but there was no criminal intent. It is simply that the registration failed. In that case there would be nothing fiktiv at all. The money would simply disappear into the bank. Possibly an audit could find it, possibly not. That is, the first statement of the bank raises a fear that the system of registration was faulty; there is no criminal and there is no fiction. There is only a slippage; money changes hands and leaves a trace to only one of the parties. The money would not disappear from the memory of the owner but he would no longer have possession of "his" money. I put "his" in quotes because money that disappears in that way no longer belongs to anyone. For instance, even if the same bills were found, there would be nothing to indicate ownership. One suspects, without ever being able to know with confidence, that there, on the computer, the money evaporated. Not the money itself, which continues to circulate in the bank and eventually outside it, but the valid trace of the money. The malfunctioning computer marks the place of disappearance of all traces. Nonetheless the effects of disappearance persist.

One can find an equivalent for the malfunctioning computer in traditional Java. There is a form of ghost called a *tuyul,* a spirit who steals. Tuyul are sometimes in the control of certain individuals and sometimes not. They are invoked when the disappearance of an object seems unaccountable, as with the malfunctioning computer. But sometimes the story is elaborated: So and so has a tuyul working for him. At that point one can see a fiction arise comparable to the story of the practitioners of the fictiv in the story of the bank. The object is left in memory but seems to have disappeared from the world. Were it to reappear it might be because the tuyul left it somewhere; or it might be because the person who controls the tuyul put it there after receiving it from the tuyul. At that point, the spirit is not important any longer. What matters is the thief.

At the point where objects disappear and where ownership itself becomes problematic, one senses a power at work. But this power is only implied in the stories of *Tempo*. Tuyul belong to a world populated with a large number of well-defined spirits.[2] People who live in this world are used to the workings of ghosts and invoke them easily enough, though with an emphasis of some sort, at least in my experience hearing these stories. By contrast, *Tempo* and, for that matter, *Pos Kota,* do not yet have a comparable idiom. In my opinion, the interest of the stories is located in the implication that behind the events there is "something." Perhaps the converse is more accurate. Stories arise against a possibility of a disappearance so complete that no trace remains. Once the site of that disappearance—computers, ghosts—is established stories can arise. That there is not or not yet a general word for the something comparable to ghost is what allows *Pos Kota* to repeat the same stories (with only details and initials changed) year in and year out, without readers losing interest. *Tempo,* on the other hand, finds new stories. In both cases, the interest is in the power of expression that can be found at the limit of the social world.

The question that raises itself here is why the idiom changes. Why is it that today there are stories of the palsu or the fiktiv, stories of criminals, whereas before there were stories of ghosts? Of course, the contrast is not absolute; thieves existed before and ghosts certainly continue to exist in the Indonesian world. But there is a sense in which one replaces the other.

If there is, in both cases, a power located at the limit of the social world, that limit has changed. Ghosts haunt, which means that they inhabit certain places. The range of their travel is restricted. They remain within the village or the region. But the palsu belongs to the nation. As such it finds its own places of disappearance or haunted sites—computers, for instance—in a register that belongs to the national and, indeed, the international.

But the question of why ghosts have, to a degree, been replaced with the palsu and, for that matter, with the criminals of kriminalitas, has another element. There remains the question of why there should be this nameless power, designated only negatively by the palsu, which invests Indonesia. If the counterfeit were simply accepted, so that there was no idea of the palsu, one would have difficulty noticing that there is something ghostly in Indonesian national culture. But the eagerness not merely to produce counterfeits, but to expose them, and to expose them gleefully and with good nature, indicates a feeling that something wants to make itself felt. Whatever that something is, it breaks into awareness only inadequately, the way a ghost makes itself felt only as a presence that is not altogether here, that belongs as much to another realm.

To explain why such a feeling should not only be pervasive, but celebrated as an element of national culture rather than, for instance, the urge an individual might have to write something, we turn back to Sukarno standing before "the people." Those in the stadium or hearing the president over the radio are transformed into "the people" as they feel that they are making their presence known. They are part of the Indonesian nation but many of them are at home listening to their radios or in villages perhaps before a communal receiver. They might not even have had the opportunity to hear the broadcast; they may only have heard of it. But the result is the same. They are part of the rakyat.

This change of identity is as abrupt as the appearance of MK who comes through the door into the living room, knife in hand, to kill his unsuspecting uncle. But it is not the criminal who appears through Sukarno's rhetoric. The nephew remained in the identity with which he was born. He killed his uncle because, as more than his uncle, as surrogate father, the uncle did not find him a place in the wider national society. Sukarno, by contrast, did so with his rhetoric and his "revolutionary economics" even if the latter left many in the same occupational position as this nephew-unemployed. The expectation of a new identity was formed precisely on the failure of the father and the laws of kinship in general, as we have already stated. The desire that circulates in the family and that needs to be transformed for the family to remain the family, protected against incest, needs, at least in retrospect, to have a normal path of transformation.

In the New Order, it is precisely the arrival in the nation, as a member of the "people," that, for political reasons, has been blocked. But, having been blocked, it is feared to have deviated. The pressure for expression that once would have led to national membership now culminates in the palsu, placing these counterfeiters, once discovered, under the rubric kriminalitas. The palsu, based as it is on the implication of an amorphous power capable of being tapped by individuals, is false because it is individuals and not leaders such as Sukarno who claim it. Or, to put it another way, anyone who could successfully claim this power would make a place for himself in the Indonesian nation, perhaps as a rich man, perhaps as a curer, perhaps as a president.

In the absence of such, other stories arise. These are more sinister than the palsu reverting as they do to monstrosities.

Some Criminal Types

Pos Kota repeats the same themes without fear of boring its readers. *Tempo*, on the other hand, looks for variety. It is not less concerned with the power of criminals than *Pos Kota*. But it has another strategy for evoking it. *Tempo* looks for the production of oddities. Criminals, in *Tempo*, often turn out to be freakish.

Though *Tempo* is read mainly in cities and mainly by the middle class, under kriminalitas it reported crimes from anywhere in Indonesia where they might find anomalies. There are many reports from villages. Villagers in their presentations are uneducated or poorly educated, the targets of "development," one of the key words of the New Order. Such people are *bodoh,* meaning stupid but capable of being enlightened. They are material for the nation but they need to be educated in order to develop their potential not merely as citizens in the political sense but as people whose horizons are those of the nation and who act in terms of a national identity. They are far from being contemptible, all the more since they are implicitly earlier versions of *Tempo*'s readers. As such, there is a commonality that leads to thinking about how they act even if they are monstrous. Here is an example:

> Murder: The Story of Muralam, the Poor Murderer Marulam was terrified: How could it be that he could crush three human heads. This is not a story of cruelty. Mad or sane, which the court will later declare, society does not want to take back this poor murderer. (*Tempo,* 16 July 1983: 34–35)

The story takes place in a Sumatran village, Desa Pasar Simangambat. A boy in the second grade shows up with a head wound. He had disappeared; villagers had thought he was in the clutches of a *machluk,* a (supernatural) creature with long hair. But the creature turns out to be their fellow villager, Muralam. The body reports that Muralam attacked him and another boy, eight years old. The other boy was killed. The boys were playing in the river when Muralam appeared and invited them to go fishing with him further up the river, in the jungle. Then he took out an axe and struck. When he was arrested, "that very afternoon," Muralam confessed not only to the murderous attacks but also to killing his good friend Dirman the year before. Villagers had thought Dirman, too, had been attacked by the creature with long hair and were so afraid that they seldom ventured into the woods and never went out after dark.

Muralam faces a possible death sentence. But this does not prevent him from answering questions about the crimes.

> The man with the sharp eyes did not try and conceal his work to the judge, Muchtar Ritonga. He gave his answers with great facility. In fact, he was surprised, 'I already confessed to the police. Now they ask me again?' he said during the court session.

He is not afraid of the consequences, perhaps because he does not understand them. But he speaks clearly, thus it is not evident that he is mad. Instead he is poor, implying here that he is bodoh as well. Like the child murderers, he does not know enough to be properly afraid of the police, the courts, and so on. Though he has other fears. When it thunders, a villager tells *Tempo,* he puts his head in a sack and hides under the bed. And he can wet his pants when he sees someone in a green or yellow uniform, that is, a policeman or a soldier. But, Muralam himself tells the reporter, now that he is in prison he has gotten used to it. "I am not terrified any more."

It is a question of values. He overvalues natural forces, not understanding their proper place, just as he overvalues the power of the police and the army. He lives in the presence of great forces, which he seems to amalgamate: There is a threatening power that passes in the road in the form of a policeman or in thunder. And he does not understand its relation to him, that it can be mediated, for instance. He thus does not see that once he has told the police, it is not the same thing as telling the judge. To tell one is to tell the other, in his mind. He does not see the value of his words. He does not know enough not to confess to a murder no one had accused him of. For him, to be asked is to reply not merely without evasion but with more than was asked for; he feels "they" want to know. Again he speaks lucidly, and what he says is taken as factual; were he to lie he would control his speech himself. But he dares not, even when his life is at stake. His speech is controlled by the power who asks the question. Were he to take that power for himself, he might have become a counterfeiter.

It is difficult to judge his sanity precisely because he is lucid and accurate in his account. But his reactions are completely out of proportion. Thus, asked why he killed his friend Dirman, he replies:

"Because he was always talking with my wife." So, apparently, he was jealous.

Tempo can understand the problem. Jealousy is something that happens to everyone. Marulam is like us, not different, in his sensibilities. But he is different in his reactions. Asked why he killed the eight-year-old Makruf, he replies:

> "I hate Lobe Harun, his grandfather." The story is that once he went to Lobe who was the head of Simangambat Village and asked for an identity card. His request was denied because, though he lived in that village [Simangambat Village], Marulam officially was registered as a member of [another village]. Ever since then, he confessed, he had it in for Lobe. The only thing was, every time he tried to do something, "It was me instead of him who got scared."

He has no identity card and he cannot get one for reasons he does not understand. He asks for one from the headman of the village where he lives. But, for the purposes of the state, he does not live there; he lives elsewhere. All he needed to do was to go to Bunungtua Pandaptona Village where, at least if things went as they should, he would have no trouble getting an identity card. He does not understand the difference between himself in his corporeal person and himself as inscribed in the books of the state. He goes unrecognized in his actual person and he does not understand how to take on his state-ascribed identity for himself. Were he to understand the difference, he would not have been filled with rage and, what is more important to us, with fear. He would have seen that the state recognizes him in a limited sense. As it is, he assumes he is completely transparent to them and speaks accordingly. They ask him a question, he tells them everything he knows.

Given his condition, he cannot respond in such a way as to get what he wants, neither an identity card nor the elimination of the man who refuses to give him the card. He tries, but he is filled with incomprehension and terror. He therefore murders a little boy, the grandson of the man he hates. He murdered the other boy by mistake. He thought he was someone else, a boy who had bothered his daughter who "several months later died of dysentery." *Tempo*'s suggestion is that in the mind of Marulam, his daughter's death from dysentery and whatever it was the boy did are related. His response is murder. Of course there is no connection between whatever relation the boy had with his daughter and her death by disease. It is one more example of bodoh, "unrelieved ignorance." It shows this original stupidity to be the opposite of the talent needed to function in society. One learns how to behave; if one does not learn, the result is not merely improper behavior; it is a relation to power that both terrorizes and leads to terrorizing others.

Muralam shows that one can be asocial and never so appear. In the village he was not known for being cruel (*buas*) or disruptive. Rather, he spent much time by himself, going off into the forest to hunt for wood which he sold to support his family. He is the poorest farmer of the village. He has three children but, Marulam tells *Tempo*, he had thirteen. The other ten died one after the other until he thought they had been bewitched. It is his poverty and not his character that is at fault. Less poor, he would understand more; understanding more he would act rightly.

As it turned out, he threatens further disruption. Whether he is thought insane or sane, if he is released the villagers have decided they will not take him back.

> "Frankly, the people of Simangamant and the villages around it want vengeance (dendam). It could well happen that if he gets out, someone else will take his place in prison," said Rafli Simatupang, the head of Urbatua Village next to Simangambat Village—whether as a threat or out of fear.

Muralam shows the urgent necessity for development, for guided evolution out of ignorance and stupidity. In the absence of such, in poverty, there is not merely material misery, there is a misunderstanding of power that sets off vengeance and thus threatens the operations of the state.

Muralam can stand as an example of a type implicitly generated in the pages of *Tempo*, the bodoh, which we can now translate as both stupid and undeveloped. This type is well elaborated. I will give one more example, the report of a soldier who wanted to take a second wife. (*Tempo*, 9 April 1983: 57–58; Pembunuhan: Prajurit Mata Gelap) When the second woman heard her lover was already married, she wrote him a letter urging him to return to his wife and child who, she said, needed him. But this letter, ending their love, according to *Tempo* "brought catastrophe to Bestina" (the wife). It was this that decided Bernard Sihombing, her husband, to murder her. Bernard defended himself in the military court in which he was tried. But *Tempo*, which as usual gives views of his guilt and innocence, notes that Bernard showed no sense of loss when Bestina was missing. He did not report her missing to his superiors; he could not prove where he was when the murder was committed. These are errors that reason shows any innocent person would have avoided, but also any person with a degree of craft. Bernard, in the report, is pictured as without the enlightenment that would lead to intelligent evasiveness. These comments, which amount to saying that "If I were Bernard. . . . I, as innocent, would have felt the loss," or "I, the enlightened murderer, would have contrived an alibi." The military prosecutor amplifies this view of the criminal as savage. Letkol M. Thaher said, "This is the most despicable [*terkeji*] murder ever committed by a military man." In the eyes of the prosecutor, a soldier should have a higher standard of behavior. He should only kill under certain circumstances and never as Bernard is alleged to have killed. Bernard, deciding to rid himself of his wife, exceeded reasonable limits. "The murder of Bestina Silalahi, twenty years old, was indeed *sadis*," comments *Tempo*. Not only was she stabbed repeatedly and her body disfigured, but she was raped by three of Bernard's friends before she was murdered. Sadis is a term derived from sadistic, which began to appear widely after the change of regime.[3]

To the prosecutor, Bernard, and to *Tempo*, the murderer (whoever he was), exceeded the limits of national reason. A military man, said the prosecutor (meaning, I am certain, an Indonesian military man), never before had done such a thing. Bernard's own defense followed a similar line of argument:

> "Its slander," he said with rage. "What husband could bear to see his wife raped and then kill her?"

Bernard invokes not the military but the normality of the family. The outrageousness of the crime is his defense. Thus both prosecution and defense invoke the norms of an institution, and institutions of a certain type. The military is national. But the family, in the sense that Bernard invoked it, is the same. He does not, for instance, rely on the customs of the Batak, the ethnic group to which he belongs judging by his name, but on the family, an understanding of which is national. He is a soldier and a husband. Normally, neither would act as he was accused of acting. But in his case, there is a new sort of criminal. He has done something unprecedented. And it is not certain what prompted him to do so.

What is at stake here is a perverted development. As someone emerging from the village, someone with military training, Bernard should not have been a criminal. But whatever moved him came from outside the usual things that move people to be criminals. One can say that he was in love and that this is scarcely a new story. But *Tempo* sees even this as strange:

> Bestina [Bernard's wife], with her yellowish brown skin, in fact was prettier and younger than Rostina [the other woman]. But for some unknown reason Bernard, from the time he met Rostina, 24, often fought with his wife.

Tempo might have found Bernard understandable if Rostina had been prettier and a few years younger. Then she would be the type that any man might fall in love with after comparison with his wife. But Bernard is strange because he was attracted to someone whom *Tempo*, presumably with the eye not of every man, but every Indonesian (since only Indonesians would know the value of '*kulit kuning langsat;* "yellowish brown skin") found less attractive. In the world of *Tempo*, there is a gradation of position, wealth, and beauty that defines the Indonesian world. It has its own vocabulary (yellowish brown skin) and standards (age of women, for instance). Crime is placed within these standards. One might murder for love of a woman everyone finds attractive; but to be sadis is to express one's urges with extreme violence because they arise outside the normal. Bernard is not understandable; this is confirmed by his strange judgments, which, *Tempo* implies, match no one else's. It is in this way that *Tempo* constantly generates new criminal types. Law breakers whose motivations are not ours are, therefore, unreasonable. The sadis is but one example.

The sadis is common to both village and city. But the village in the reports of *Tempo* yields a particular sort of criminal. Like the men discussed earlier, he is one who does not understand national norms. They connect this failure to learn with poverty. The unnatural type is the effect of an inability to see the proper relation of values to one another, poverty being not merely material but also moral deprivation.

We could label another category of lawbreaker "criminal children." Thus *Tempo* has a story under this headline:

> Child Murder (#2)
> Nurdian, The Unfortunate Little One.
> 3 minors kill a friend they are playing with, only because they want earrings. They are not held, but returned to their parents. The police ask for a psychiatrist's help. (*Tempo*, 28 May 1983: 62)

In Den Pasar, the capital city of Bali, a four-year-old girl was murdered while playing with three friends who "held [her] up with a weapon." When she cried, her playmates held her mouth shut, strangled her, and hit her on the head with a club. They cut off her ears and stole her earrings. That afternoon the other three came back and threw the body in a river.

Neighbors reported the girl missing to the police. The police were led to the others, the ringleader of whom was a twelve-year-old girl, when one of the three raved in her sleep, repeating the cries for mercy of the little girl. Eventually the neighbors reported the girl missing to the police and the three children, twelve, ten, and nine years old, were brought in. The twelve-year-old, a girl, was said to be *nakal* (said of someone, particularly a child, who misbehaves), and confessed to being the ringleader while the other two just did as she told them.

The earrings, worth Rp15,000, were sold for Rp6,500, and the money was divided: Wayan, Rp4,000, Abdillah Rp1,500, Ubaidillah Rp1,000.

> Because their confession was considered sufficient, the suspects were sent back to their parents, who, since the case broke, were 'secured' [against revenge] so their houses are empty. The reason given for their return is that the suspects are underage. Will they be brought to trial?

It's not certain. The police are seeking the advice of a psychiatrist. Meanwhile an atmosphere of mourning (*duka*) pervades the housing complex that opened just six months earlier. There is a patrol every night. "Who knows if someone will try and take revenge?"

Once again there is a crime done for incomprehensible reasons that leads to feelings of revenge. It seems to be a particularly incomprehensible crime that sets off threats of vengeance. It is incomprehensible in this case because the criminals are children who act like adults. On the one hand they are "mischievous," a quality especially that of children. But on the other there is the seriousness of their crime and, at least as important, that it was committed for gain, in the manner of adults. Though murder for gain is understandable, murder for so little gain and murder by children is not. These children act like adults. They steal what adults steal—jewelry. And they sell the loot for money and divide the spoils by merit, like adults. They are thus a mirror of the adult community. But they remain outside not only the law, but outside comprehension. Are they insane? Are they disturbed? That is, is there a category for them? In every way but age they are adults, responding to the same idiom of desire—money—as adults.

Indonesian children often wear gold earrings and other gold jewelry. These ornaments are not exactly toys; their loss is usually thought of as severe. There are a number of reports, in *Pos Kota* especially, of poor women who lure little girls into places where they can be safely relieved of their jewelry. The intersection of the want of the poor and the luxury of children, at least certain children, creates the drama of these pieces. Sometimes these are women on the edge of starvation or whose own children are hungry. It is not necessarily a class question; even families of quite modest means might well give their daughters gold jewelry. It is a form of savings. The child is like a bank; her very youth means that the gold is put away for a time of necessity, if not for her marriage. Stories of their theft by adults bring children themselves, as victims, into the world of adults before their maturity.

In this story, children are brought into the adult world as victims and as criminals. As criminals they reflect doubt on themselves and the adult world. When these murderous children kill for gold earrings they demonstrate that they want what adults want. The miniaturization of children's objects that makes them attractive and amusing to adults is not at work here. The earrings are gold, worth the same as any other pieces of gold of the same weight. These children are in the same trajectory of desire as adults. That alone might make them monstrous. As children, their wants should be unsettled. They should be easily distracted, as children are reputed to be. But as reported by *Tempo* their determination to have what they want, their steadiness of focus, and the complexity of their actions are not childish.

One might say that they demonstrate the natural or universal value of gold; it appeals even to those who have yet to learn its true value. And yet most adults would not have killed for it. The gap between the naturalness of attraction and the act of appropriation makes these children monstrous. Adults who murder only for a pair of earrings might be equally monstrous. But children are more so, because the crime demonstrates the force of attraction of gold to be more powerful, of wider scope of appeal, than its "natural" value. It threatens the very naturalization of appeal that one relies on. Gold is valuable; one saves it, counts on its continued value to be useful later. It is the very reason to give little girls gold earrings. And yet the force of its attraction is such that humans kill for it. The possibility of its integration into the heart of social life, mediating as it does buying and selling as well as marriage exchange gives society a reliable reference point. Here this reference is challenged. Gold appears too powerful, capable of turning children into adults before their time, upsetting fundamental (and naturalized) categories of social life.

When children murder "only for a pair of earrings" it makes it seem that the difficulty is both children and gold.[4] Given the possibility of this imbalance in the force that should make for social harmony, it remains to put a face on those labeled as criminal. A frequently cited case is that of rich adolescents. In a report on adolescent crime, *Tempo* says that apparently it is increasing. "On every side there are indeed thefts and break-ins committed by youth. Maybe they are incited by the desire to follow adolescent life styles today."⁵ Thus, a robbery of a pharmacy in Kabanjahe, North Sumatra, in which Rp700,000 plus lots of valium were stolen. Only when one of the teenage boys was arrested after an accident on his motor bike and was found to be sedated did the robbery come to light. This is cause for incredulity. The police commandant "almost did not believe it."

> If they stole a chicken to make *saté*, maybe one could forgive them. But this?

It is a question of the "life style" (*gaya hidup*) of adolescents. Many "can restrain themselves" in the face of it, but others cannot. In Jakarta, a teenager robs and kills a taxi driver. This teenager was the head of a gang that robbed for excitement. He and his gang are arrested in the midst of a robbery and end in a line-up. He is a good student.

The former undesirable activities of adolescents—skipping school, fighting—are now said to be dated (*kuno*). The problem is that adolescent criminality is mounting, though *Tempo* is unclear about this. In any case, they report a police officer who classifies them in two groups. There are those who act spontaneously, without reflection. And then there are others who

> are accustomed to antisocial actions and continue to the world of crime (kejahatan). . . . If they are not quickly controlled, "they have a tendency to become recidivists."

It is the recidivists who are feared. These criminals escape reform. Many articles are devoted to the failure of prison to cleanse criminals of their criminal habits. These are the people who develop in another direction entirely, escaping development.

Again there is an institutional failure. A student at the Law Faculty of the University of Indonesia states that such students are without parental supervision. It is a question of the middle class; those already part of national development. But in the heart of the institution that should be a sign of successful national development there is a breakdown.

This family is itself correctable. It needs only to awaken the parents. This law student—he is not an expert, but merely intends to be one—cites a case where the father was a sailor, therefore away from home, and the mother went out nearly every night, "no one knows where." The adolescent criminal in this case led a gang that robbed houses in the neighborhood. The houses "of acquaintances of the parents or of neighbors. These friends would give *informasi*—when a house was left empty, the inhabitants leaving town with only a servant left behind—and could be robbed." Furthermore, they robbed when they were drunk. The parents never knew about it. In another case reported by this same law student, a gang of adolescents started to steal cars. At first it was casual, simply a question of demonstrating to others how one of the boys could open a locked car in a minute. The boy did not want to say where he learned to do so. The next steps were taken by others who were already "professionals." With the money, he would treat his friends, who would drink until they were drunk. And not only that. He would rent a hotel room for two or three days, in a three-star hotel, and invite pretty girls.

> You don't believe it? At first I myself could not imagine (juga tidak mengira) there was such a model of adolescent life.

This law student is writing a book on the topic. "Apparently he wants to turn on a yellow light for us," comments *Tempo*.

Much occurs in discotheques, but particularly discotheques in the grand hotels of Jakarta, those intended for and usually owned or operated by foreign concerns. These are costly. In an accompanying article, which is only partly about criminals (Gaya Hidup 'Wah', Tapi Bukan Kriminal, 71–72), *Tempo* reports on the large amount of money commanded by upper class kids; one has Rp270,000 a month in spending money, credit cards, and the like.

Here it is money and foreignness that seems to corrupt youth. But it is a mistake to see this as the singular source of criminality. *Tempo* frequently raises cases where they point, as in the case of the sergeant, to the unknown motivation. Doubtless they rely on a positivist psychologizing to discover the ultimate basis of such crimes. But in continually proposing new criminal types, they raise questions of motivation, one could say, "the" question of motivation, and seldom reach a conclusion.

One sees in their accounts two elements. First are the new sorts of criminal whose "sadism" seems invariably to be a way of indicating the presumably unfathomable motivations of criminals. Second are various sources, as one might name them, for criminals. In this instance, it is the high spending ways of adolescents. They impress each other, copy each other, need money for their pleasures, and so on. But each time it is a question of seeing them, the criminals, as failed Indonesians. Criminals again respond to something other than the formation they have received as citizens, something that makes them incredible according to police, sociologists, and ordinary citizens. One cannot believe they are like that.

Because as Indonesians it is incomprehensible not merely that Indonesian institutions should not hold, but that there should be other sources of motivation than that furnished by the nation. It is at the point of articulation between family and nation that failure is located. A criminal such as Muralam remains locked in a prenational world or fails to interiorize national values, as in the case of the soldier who murdered his wife. The family is charged with a national duty, to form children to be citizens. And too often they fail.

There is a further element. These criminals, although ultimately incredible, are nonetheless fathomable to a certain extent. One can understand the attractions of certain criminality. Take, for instance, the word "top"; it is from English, and it refers to the best, the most expensive. It is used for the foreign hotels where the best discotheques are found; the top houses that certain criminals in Jogjakarta are said to have built, as we shall see in the next chapter.

One is left with two sources of criminality. There is the unfathomable criminal who is, ipso facto, a monster, the sadis, for instance, who responds to something no one can recognize. And there is the person who wants just what everyone else does. But in achieving his wishes he becomes a criminal and often a monster. Child murderers are the example we cited.

The effect of creating monsters, as pictured in *Tempo* and, for that matter, *Pos Kota*, is the creation of rumor. Take this example from *Tempo* entitled:

> Between the girl and the long haired (boy): Here is a picture of kriminalitas in the capital. A student from a senior technical high school is accused of killing a kid. In whose hands Iis's necklace has ended up is unclear. (*Tempo*, 19 December 1992: 94)

"Here is a picture of kriminalitas," meaning that this story somehow has the essence of kriminalitas. Why is not specified in the report.

A nine-year old girl, Iis, is found in a lane late one afternoon, her head bloody, in agony. A youth says he has found a piece of wood wrapped in a blood-stained newspaper not far away. He claims, without saying how he knows, that the piece of wood was thrown out by Phinia, the student accused of murder, as Iis died shortly after being found. Before her death, she repeats the name, Phinia, even though otherwise she is comatose. She is from a poor family, her mother being a laundress and her father a trishaw driver. Phinia herself disappears. She has gone to the National Monument. The next day she is arrested. She was seen carrying the girl in her arms an hour before the girl was found wounded. What *Tempo* finds puzzling is the motive. The public prosecutor says Phinia wanted the girl's necklace, which weighed two grams. But the necklace cannot be found. The girl's mother is certain that Phinia is guilty. What makes her certain is the necklace. Phinia's desire for it was so great that she became incensed (*mata gelap*) and killed the little girl. She wanted the necklace for its monetary value; but that value by itself would be too small to account for murder. It is rather that her desire drove her into a state of fury and in that state she killed.

But at the same time, one cannot be sure that it was Phinia or that if it was it was because of the necklace. The necklace is said to be essential to establishing Phinia's guilt. If it were in someone else's hands, it might exonerate Phinia. Or if Phinia had it it would indicate her guilt. But it might still not explain how it is that she became enraged enough to kill.

Many people in the neighborhood are convinced that Phinia killed Iis. It is on the basis of her character:

> Phinia was known to be mischievous (nakal), to have a spectacular life style (hidup wah) and to be addicted to forbidden drugs. People say her father, Mursid Rum, an army veteran, remarried. The daily expenses of Phinia and her 4 siblings were paid out of the pocket of the oldest.

Phinia has a bad reputation; more precisely, she is said to live adventurously and to take drugs. In this sense she fits our description of criminals as people who respond to other attractions than those holding the attention of law-abiding citizens. Her father is respectable, but he, a retired soldier, has abandoned his responsibilities. The implication is that the father does not exercise control. The result again is that his daughter is not amenable to the same messages, the same thoughts, as her neighbors.

But this formulation raises charges of slander and gossip:

> Mursyid said the accusations against his daughter were the purest slander, manufactured by those who did not like her. 'I was once the neighborhood head here,' he said.

He and the defense attorney say that the prosecutor has merely imagined Phinea's activities at the time of the murder. Phinia claims that she saw Iis covered with blood at 4:45 and that she held the bloody piece of wood and paper. But she saw a youth at the end of the gang, was afraid of being suspected herself, and so fled. "Because she had been accused of all kinds of things, Phinia disappeared . . . to the National Monument."

She has not identified the youth, and it is not explained that, since she was already recognized, it would do no good to flee. Also the prosecutor found the same blood on her cap, which she left in the public transport she took, as on the piece of wood.

> Does Phinia have a strong alibi? Or can she and her attorney produce Mister X, the long-haired youth? Here is a picture of criminal behavior (kriminalitas) in the capital.

The report ends with the same assertion of typicality contained in the headline. For *Tempo,* it is a question of who to believe. And this question rests on understanding a certain situation: The neighbors suspect her because of her character; she knows that she is suspected before she has done anything. And she uses that knowledge as a defense.

It is typically "kriminalitas in the capital" because, for *Tempo,* it is a question of who to believe. That question involves her character as it is known in the neighborhood and, beyond that, the use she herself makes of what people think of her. If she is believable, it is despite what people think about her. She builds their knowledge of her into her defense. She flees the neighborhood, she says, because she knows what people say about her and therefore is afraid that she will be charged. She wants the court to believe her because she is aware that she is thought disreputable. Her socially anomalous position becomes her defense. People might think she ran away because she was guilty. But they should believe her; she ran away because she knew she would be thought guilty.

If she is believable, then there is a truth that does not depend on character but instead on understanding how certain types incite rumor and how these types, knowing that, act accordingly. She wants the court to believe her despite what people say even if they speak the truth about her character. She makes two claims: the first we have already stated, that she knows what they say about her and acts accordingly. The second is that the court should believe her despite the fact that it is she, Phinia the bad girl, that speaks. There is always the possibility of reading not character but a certain situation, a structure. She claims to speak not as "Phinia" in Phinia's interest, but as someone who understands how gossip works. Phinia knows how those who are anomalous are talked about, how they know it, how they act upon this knowledge. Phinia the bad girl can step outside the identity she and others have created for her and which has stimulated the circulation of rumors. She can describe how rumor works out of her own experience. The foundation of belief in her is her reflection on herself.

Kriminalitas we have seen is based on the incredible. It is the appearance of what you would never believe. And now it speaks for itself out of the mouth of one of those typical of her kind. The monstrous, the snatcher of children's jewelry, the Indonesian adolescent who is too strongly attracted to what money buys; Phinia is said to be all of these. She does not deny her bad reputation, the use of drugs, the adolescent way of life. She simply denies that it led to murder. And yet to believe her one has to believe that she speaks as someone who accepts her monstrosity. She is guilty of other crimes, not this one. It is exactly from her position outside of ordinary structures of belief that she makes a claim. It would only be just. This differs from the justice of the prosecutor who, it is implied, relies partly on evidence, but, the evidence being incomplete, also on character, that is, on what people say. The justice of the state, in this case, is the possibility of making rumor truth. The justice claimed by monstrosity would say that, whatever the court decides, Phinia is innocent. Those who incarnate the incredible nonetheless can speak the truth; they, via Phinia, claim a place for themselves.

If the incredible is nonetheless possibly to be believed, the state could profit from it. It could take the position of impartial justice. In this instance, it coopts rumor; rumor has nothing to say that the state cannot accept. Alas, we do not know how the case was decided. But if the prosecutor got his way, the incredible was condemned. It could not win recognition once again.

The fear of the state and perhaps of the nation is precisely that the incredible will be believed. That is implicit in the reports of counterfeiting. One may not believe it, but the money in your hand was made by your neighbor. The incredible is present; the difficulty is to keep it in place, that is, out of circulation. To put it another way, Phinia's character attracts attention; people gossip. Her arrest and trial are a form of state recognition of this circulation. The monstrous was present even before the murder; the trial and the report of the trial links rumor into a national trajectory that is under the control of the state. All rumor returns to the center even or perhaps especially that of the incredible, there to be put under control.

Against this would be a form of recognition that would not depend on the state. It would claim that even if guilty in the court, Phinia is innocent. This claim depends on monstrosity making its own trajectory, one that would go beyond the gossip that already circulated about Phinia. Phinia would force others to recognize the truth of what she said while never denying what people know about her. She would achieve recognition equal to that given in the law court. Hers is the claim of monstrosity to show up and to be granted a place not out of previously existing standards of truth, but out of its very power to make itself felt. "The people" then, would live again, forcing their way on their own, without a leader such as Sukarno.

Further Kriminalitas: Sadis and Incest

Against the possibility represented by Phinia there is another. To see it, we have to look at some more stories. Here is one that appeared in *Pos Kota* on 23 October 1979. It contains the elements of many others on the same theme. A man, forty-four, from a Javanese town, makes his own daughter pregnant. When the girl's mother was three months pregnant with her, she left the father. After the girl was three years old, she was sent to live with her father. The rape occurred after the girl reached adolescence. The father "could not contain his desire [*nafsu*], especially one night when he saw Sth. [the daughter] sprawled out asleep." The report describes how the father restrained his daughter and raped her. "Because she was threatened and frightened, Sth. acquiesced." Their relations continued until Sth. was eight months pregnant. The father found someone to marry his daughter, giving the man Rp25,000 to do so. The baby died. After a year and a half of marriage the couple divorced, the girl went back to her father and he once more made her pregnant. This time, in her eighth month, ashamed, she fled, and told someone what happened; that someone reported the story to the police. The police arrested the father and he was sentenced to eighteen months in jail minus time served.

Pos Kota here reports a case from the courts; it is part of the scandal, the headline reading "Father Rapes Daughter Twice: Only Sentenced to 18 Months." In these stories of incest, it is always the fault of the parent, usually the father. It is the case, too, with rape: The man is always at fault. In other societies where awareness of women's rights is as little developed as in Indonesia one might find the woman accused of overstimulating the man.

Pos Kota has an occasional column where, instead of waiting for events to reach them, they look into certain conditions. A favorite topic is prostitutes; how certain women come to be prostitutes, what their families think, and so on. One of these series concerned those who live together outside marriage. They found certain of them among the homeless, in particular those who sleep under bridges. These reports, too, were concerned with incest, even though the families reported were constructed without marriage. Take for instance, the family described in "Living Together Under a Bridge: The Unfortunate Si Siti, Victim of Her Father's

Savage Desire" (23 October 1983). Here the girl states that her father seduced her, she came to like it and found a boyfriend of her own with whom to continue, again outside marriage. The reporter is shocked, asks whether such cases are common and answers himself. "Who knows. . . . ! ! ! But it is clear that there are a lot of illegitimate children among those who simply do as they like." The effect of incest most deplored by the reporter is, in fact, illegitimacy.

In another article in the series ("Child forced to Serve Her Father, Pregnant 5 Months, Mother Flees, Unable to Stand the Suffering"; 16 October 1983) the reporter fears that living together outside marriage, which in several places he conflates with incest, will result in a major increase in the numbers of illegitimate children. He suggests that such people need guidance and education and that they should join the transmigrants clearing fields in the jungle. Otherwise, "is it not the case that in a short time to come, ten years, it is not impossible that the numbers of people born from then will increase further." The illegitimate will keep appearing.

There are many similar stories. Sometimes they are not actually incestuous but incest is suggested. This is the case when a servant is raped by her boss or someone in the family. The servant is often said to be "a member of the family," augmenting the scandal. In the previous report there are only the father and daughter in the household. Where there are others, the crime is usually said to take place in the absence of some adult. A report in the same issue of *Pos Kota* as that just quoted has this headline:

> The Son of the Boss Stains the Servant who Disappears in the 7th month of the Pregnancy. It Has Already Been Reported to the Kebayoran Police (Kebayoran is a section of Jakarta).

The servant was seduced in the absence of the boy's father. She expected him to marry her. When he did not, she ran off. She could not go home out of shame. She told a peddlar who reported the incident to the police. It is again implied that the presence of the father would have meant the impossibility of the seduction. And once again *Pos Kota* is quite precise about the way the news reached the police. It is seldom the victim who reports to the police; nearly always it is a third party.

Pos Kota is always interested to know how the news got out of the house and then to the police. Under the headline "His Own Child Raped Till She is Pregnant. He is Finally Shut up in Jail" (25 October 1979) there is the story of a father and mother who had decided to sleep in different beds. He, therefore, slept with his sixteen-year-old daughter. When she was well pregnant the mother was told about it by the girl's younger sibling. The family, it is said, went to the police, implying not the mother herself but some member of her family.

In the story entitled "Own Child and Brother-in-law's Daughter Are Victims of Savage Sexuality" ("Anak Kandung Dan Adik Ipar Jadi Korban Keganasan Sex," *Pos Kota*, 2 November 1979) a father sleeps with his daughter. The daughter complains to her mother that her vagina is sore. The mother brings her to a doctor. The story comes out and the mother sets a trap. In the middle of the night, the husband tells her he is going to go their daughter's bed. The mother agrees, waits, then, seeing what happens and filled with disgust, she catches them in the act. The difficulty is that the father is oversexed, to the point where his wife gave him permission to sleep with other women. In fact, he had slept with an older daughter, now married. And he had slept with a younger one also, but the mother had gotten magical medicine that she thought controlled him.

The mother states that she does not know everything that happens in the house. She works as a baby sitter and is often gone. This time, shocked, she waited, reflected, and then reported to the person in charge of the affairs of her block, who reported to his superior, who told the police. The police officer said that this was

> the worst case he ever handled so long as he had been a police officer. "Imagine. Victimizing two of your own children," Lieutenant Djoemali stated.

Once again, there is a superlative: "the worst" of all his experiences in the police, because it is sexuality directed at one's own children. He asks his interlocutor to imagine it because it is so difficult to imagine. It is again the appearance of the incredible. Here the incredible is named. It is the superfluous sexual energy of the father, already noted by the mother who had tried to control it in different ways. She seems to have treated it as a medical problem, that is, with medicine, albeit magical medicine. In any case, the father's sexuality is surprisingly detached from his character. Thought of as a form of energy divorced from personality, he has his wife's permission to find other women. The *alat vital*, or "vital organ," the word *Pos Kota* uses for the sexual organ of either sex, has a life of its own. One need not bring the personality of the father into the picture. It is never the case that it is the victim's fault; the sight of his daughter sprawled out asleep may have aroused her father, but there is absolutely no hint of the woman who uses her sexuality when she should not. The interpersonal register is avoided.

What is left are a set of roles, familial and quasi-familial, and a current of sexual energy that flows through one of them. In place of character is structure. There should be a third party who supervises. It is in his or her absence that unwanted events occur. But even this is not so much a moral as a merely empirical fact. In the absence of the third who should be there to ensure that nothing happens is another third party, the one who finds out afterwards. Finally someone says something and eventually someone reports to the police. The police here are not sinister surveyors of what should be private. They do not survey at all; rather they act by a force of communication, as one person tells another—from the mother to the neighborhood head, from the neighborhood head to the head of that section of the city (*lurah*), and finally to the police. The police are merely the end point. When they are told, the affair is over.

There are stories where the (male) servant seduces a girl in the family. There are others where a mother seduces her son. These are much rarer than stories of fathers raping daughters. But even these stories have the disinterested quality we have already noted. A mother climbed into bed with her grown-up son in the middle of the night because it was cold. She started to rub him; it was a matter of comfort, it is implied. But then. . . . A male servant might want his bosses' daughters jewels (nonmetaphorical); it is true, but in this case, it is a matter of a swindler who then disappears, leaving the double loss of honor and wealth. There is disappointment because the servant was considered one of the family. This story edges onto the upsetting of relations of power we are familiar with in eighteenth-century Europe. But here again, the servant was one of the family, and not, therefore, merely a servant, which seems to suffice to put the question of power aside.

The violence in these stories occurs as the effect of the spontaneous arousal of desire. It is nearly always from the father or the boss or the boss's son to the daughter or the servant. Hierarchy is rarely reversed. The police are always the last resort; what one wants is for them to act sooner rather than fearing their intrusion. The difficulty with police authority is that it is not sufficiently authoritative. The difficulty with fathers is that they do not act like fathers. The wish is not to get what belongs to someone else, to imagine oneself in their place. The wish rather is that everyone remain in place; fathers should be fathers, daughters just daughters and not lovers, and servants should be "family members." The family idiom should hold.

As it is, familial categories are disturbed. The result is first "shock" (the English word is often used), then talk, then the police. Take this case:

> Wife Upset, Catches Husband Having Sex
> "Savage Brute of a Husband, . . . You Even Pick On Your Own Stepdaughter" (*Pos Kota*, 31 September 1983; Sunday)

A woman returns early from the market where she sells vegetables to find her husband having sex with his stepdaughter:

> Around dawn, the people of Cijambu, Tanjung Sari-Sumedang were suddenly startled by the hysterical (histeris) screams of Ny. Sar. In a short time neighbors flocked to the house. Ny. Sar that morning succeeded in catching her husband Sa (55) doing something filthy with her their step daughter Ning (13). She clearly could not hold back her feelings. "Savage Brute of a Husband, . . . You Even Pick On Your Own Stepdaughter," this, more or less, was what Mrs. Sar screamed making the people who lived there try and get her to calm her down and have a complaint lodged with the authorities instead, which is what happened.

She does not know why; for no reason at all, she returns home. The accident is that, prompted by something she cannot identify, she turns back and finds what she did not suspect. It is, again, the incredible, the unbelievable, outside all expectations. And yet something makes her turn back.

And there she sees the scene. But what she sees is not so clear by this stage of the report as it was earlier. Is it really incest? The girl is identified initially as their stepdaughter. But she is, again, a servant thought of as "one of the family." The girl is an orphan who they took in as a servant and whom they then considered their daughter:

> In the house of the Sar family, as well as being a servant she had become their stepdaughter.

What it means to be considered one of the family and what it means to be an adopted child are, in Java, left vague. One can be considered one of the family without anyone outside the family knowing of it. But one can also be said to be the adopted child of someone simply by the fact of close association. I, for instance, was surprised to learn that I was said to be the adopted son of a Sumatran religious scholar with whom I had close relations. An adopted child in this sense is not an heir in law, but he or she might inherit according to local custom. A girl who enters a house as a servant and has no one else to take care of her is likely to be called an adopted child; it is a question not of a formal relation but of acting in loco parentis. This girl, in any case, did not stop being a servant to take her place as their daughter. But it is not clear. The sentence in the newspaper does not necessarily point to a legal relation.

Pos Kota puts the assertion that the girl is their "adopted daughter" in quotation marks. It is the mother's assertion. She wants it to be known how heinous her husband's crime was; not merely the seduction of a servant, but incest. It is precisely what she never expected. As such, she finds a force that does more than simply divide her from her husband. Were her husband merely unfaithful, it would not attract the attention of the neighbors, the police, and *Pos Kota*. The questions of rape and seduction of servants are put in the framework of incest. As such there is a scandal that demands public attention and the action of authority.

The household, equated with the family, contains a force that it cannot control. The presence of a third party, here the wife-stepmother-employer, is necessary for there to be proper behavior. With her at home, the couple would be discovered immediately. But something goes on all the time she is there, which she is not aware of. No doubt signals are sent, evasions and denials are made, and so on. None of this registers with her, as also with the woman whose husband has already slept with two of their daughters and who agrees to his sharing a bed with a third. Nothing makes these women suspicious, no doubt because what they might suspect is too terrible to bear thinking about. But something, she does not know what, makes this market woman return home. Reading these stories one sees the strength of denial and, opposed to it, narratives structured to show family scandal poised, ready for discovery.

When such scandals are found out they take the same trajectory. There is an intervention by someone who, in another time or another context, would form part of the people; there is the peddler of soup, the person in charge of the affairs of the block, the family member, or merely someone anonymous. In *Pos Kota* these people form a link between the family struck by scandal and state authorities.

Stories of incest sometimes overlap with stories of the sadis. A man, forty-five, sleeps with his daughter, fifteen, "fully knowing what he was doing." Only after he beats his wife and she goes to the police on that account does the story come out (*Pos Kota*, 25 January 1980). We have already seen mentioned the injury done to girls' sexual organs by their fathers. *Pos Kota* does not neglect to mention this:

> Stimulated by sexual desire which boiled over as a result of the cold weather, Ng (45). . . . fornicated with K, his underage stepdaughter. As a result the girl's vital organ (alat vital) was damaged. ("Gadis di bawah umur digagahi bapak tiri," *Pos Kota*, 16 December 1983)

There are many stories of the sadis among masters who mistreat their servants, sometimes without raping them. Again these are considered particularly monstrous acts because the master (or mistress), instead of treating the servant as a member of the family, injures her.

Ratma Asks 2 Million in Damages
Servant Ironed by her Mistress
Her Body is Covered with Bruises
   (*Pos Kota,* 18 February 1983)

Boss Who Tortures Servant Lands in Prison
3 Months Work, No Wages
She Complains of the Pain When Dowsed with Hot Water
   (*Pos Kota,* 24 January 1983)

The second of these concerns a twelve-year-old girl with bruises. Her mistress, thirty-three, tortured her for two days. The sexual nature of this, which included spanking and resulted in injury to the girl's vagina, is not commented upon. Neighbors rescued the girl and then the police heard about her and arrested the woman.

There is no need for me to repeat the graphic details of these stories. It is enough to note that *Pos Kota* stresses the marks on the body of the victim. These girls come to attention with the signs of their painful experiences. Their bruises testify to their masters' and their mistresses' brutality just as the illegitimate children resulting from incest are themselves signs of an uncontrolled force that disrupts the family and calls the attention of the world to it. Stories of the sadis and of incest are alike in their structure. A disruptive force calls attention to itself; signs of this force are generated, authorities are called in, the paper reports.

In these stories servants are in the position of children, but children of a special sort. Sometimes, as in the next report, they are orphans.

Adolescent Girl Struck by Boss, Bruised
"I Can't Take it, Mister. Whats More He Wanted to Rape Me." (*Pos Kota,* 29 March 1983)

The girl is sixteen. Several times, she does not know how many times, the boss's son tries to rape her but she resists.

The climax of her suffering, Kaswan went on, was on Wednesday, 23 March 1983 when she was struck multiple times by her boss until her body was bruised in several places. Kaswan ran outside weeping.

When neighbors saw this, their hearts were moved to help the unfortunate girl. All of this was later reported to Kosek 201-01 Gambir [the name of the police station].

After Kaswan got the doctor's report at Cipto Mangungkusumo Hospital, the unfortunate girl was taken in by M. Yatiri, the head of the neighborhood organization RW.04, Keluruhan Duri Pulo, where she remains. "How could I not be moved by this girl without family in Jakarta, treated like that," said M. Yatiri, who took Kaswen to Kosek 701-01 Gambir.

There is no need to stress the repetition of the trajectory. What this story adds is the identification of the servant. She is an orphan. Not because she does not have parents, but because she is without protectors in Jakarta. It is in this sense that servants are often adopted into families. Needless to say, this does not mean that they are no longer considered daughters of their still-living original parents. But they are made orphans, even if they have parents, because in the city one has need of protection. Jakarta makes orphans of those who arrive there. The orphans of these stories are the anonymous who are in need of recognition and protection which they are expected to receive along with their jobs.

The massive assimilation of counterfeit orphans from the countryside testifies to the nation's ability to take care of its own. These, again, are those who formed the crowds that made up the people at another time. Now they take up roles in families in the narratives of *Pos Kota*. *Pos Kota* seems to be filled with success stories. These orphans who are mistreated are recognized, taken care of anyway. They arouse pity: "How could I not be moved by this girl without family in Jakarta?" One sees in them the lack of parental protection, which means that one sees in them an insufficient mark of parentage. They appear, somehow, in their very appearance, as lacking a connection with their fathers and mothers. One knows that they have come a long way, a distance great enough to make their familial bonds inoperative. They are recognized for it. They are thus close to the illegitimate, who always are seen in terms of parental bonds that are of no help to them.

The man feels pity for the orphan. He thinks of this feeling as natural; something anyone would feel. But it is someone who would see the girl not merely as mistreated and injured but as "without family in Jakarta." It is not "without family in the city," a more general statement. His phrase belongs to someone familiar with Jakarta and with the countryside as well, in short, with Indonesia. He takes the girl in; he is her provisional adoptive father. But he is that on the basis of his view of her place and his within the nation. *Pos Kota* tells these stories of criminality as stories of the rescue of less fortunate members of the nation. It is the story of the assimilative power of the nation, the absorption of those who leave remote, impoverished families, sites of unenlightened mentalities and suspicious activities.

But given the urban boss-sadis, it is equally the story of the failure of national assimilation. Making up for the failure of the nation, the police arrive. In the end it is the state that assures the proper functioning of both nation and family.

There is a force within the family or the fictive family that disrupts it, that carries shocking news outside the household, that demands to be made known and that ends with the police. In the societies that preceded the formation of the Indonesian nation there was also incest; there were orphans; there were illegitimate children. At least one thinks there were. They, however, did not lead to important or repeated stories. Where are the stories of rape, of incest in traditional Java, for instance? They are set in myth, with uncertain reference to historical realities.

Javanese society seems practically founded on disruption. One has only to read its classic ethnographies; I think, for instance, of Clifford Geertz's *The Religion of Java,* where spirits mean practically nothing other than disruption. Why, we can ask again, has the idiom of disruption changed? We have seen why. At one time law inhered in the construction of the family. When the nation declared itself to be the source of law, the family became mere custom. The traditional family is now merely customary while the Indonesian family is an effect of the nation, deriving its legitimacy and its form from outside itself. From that perspective, the household is no longer the place one goes to find someone who knows how the family should operate. That knowledge rests with enlightened nationalists. The family is a site of potential disruption. It is the site of the drive that propelled the founders of the nation to make themselves known as nationalists, a site of transgression. Sukarno slept with his mother; Kusni Kasdut's father slept with his aunt who thus became Kusni's mother. Suharto is sure people will say he is illegitimate, his parents never married.

Once the family was the source of legitimacy; now that source is outside of itself. What is revealed in the reports of the crimes of incest and sexual abuse is the force that calls for the law. There is not only the supposedly inherent disgust that incest stimulates in those who discover it. There is also the path of communication that the discovery engenders, leading as it does outside the family, to "others." It passes through these others to the police. The law and with it the state appears in response to desire.

The family is never reformed. The reason is not obvious. It might have been the case, for instance, that in the failure of the father, the rise of the sadis, the failure of the nation, the brother, the father's son, would take the role of the father. This is what has happened in Algeria for instance.[6] This result is an important component of the religious and communal struggles in that country. Indonesia seems, at least for now, to have avoided that outcome. But if so it is because of the power of the state to take the place of the father and the belief in that power that are apparent in these faits divers.

Ghosts, Criminals, and "the People"

In another era, there would have been ghosts and possession. Ghosts too call attention to themselves. They want, whatever else, to make themselves known. The criminals of the Indonesian press are not different. But the path of communication they stimulate is different. Ghosts do not end up in the hands of the state. They are dealt with by other competent authorities, ones whose relation to the nation is more ambiguous. Criminals make themselves felt, if not exactly known, just as ghosts do. But the New Order state finds itself rooted in its relation to these criminals. The path from criminals to the police leads back to criminals as well. The state becomes the agency that contains the disruption one never expected.

Ghosts are tied to particular places; they haunt their special locales. Criminals have a different locus. They are not like ghosts, because they can move from place to place. They might be found in any family in Indonesia. They are the nationalization of ghosts, as it were. But they are also the foundation of the nation today, inhering in it the way the spirits of the founders of villages remain in certain village shrines. These criminals are not, in the first place, breakers of the law. They are rather those who show the absolute necessity of the law because, once making themselves felt, and appearing the way ghosts appear, the law is bound to show up. They are the basis of legality because, by their actions, they summon the law, causing it to make its own appearance.

There is, in the structure of these narratives in the press, the necessity of a determined trajectory. But this trajectory is always in danger of having an outcome other than the one wanted. It is not because of the ineptness of the police, but because the force that drives criminality persists. It creates a society of illegitimate families, families without marriage existing under the bridges of Jakarta, breeding illegitimate children who, it is feared, will never redeem themselves. It is shown by the constant production of stories of the sadis in the form of masters and mistresses who mistreat their servant-children. Without the intervention of the police, another society or other societies would take place. Illegitimate children might not be recognized as such. Incestuous families, where children are lovers and mothers are aunts, would form themselves. It is possible that no one would be aware of it. Indonesia would be a counterfeit nation or nations. On the other hand, the suppression of these counterfeits establishes the state and thus the nation whose basis thus moves from the people to *kriminalitas*.

In the trajectory that runs from family crime, to the hearing of the crime, to the reporting of it to the police there is a certain unselfconsciousness, an ignoring of how one is seen in the eyes of others. The effective lie, says Thomas Mann, is "the product of a lively imagination" rather than a conscious deceit. It is not made with the idea of the other in mind or with the notion that one says something different from one's true intentions. In these stories, in the end, the police get the word. If one could not be sure that would be the case, perhaps a more ironic mode might develop. At that point, one would have to invent another interlocutor, putting oneself in the place of the other, seeing how one's desires, acted on, would reflect on oneself. A more self-conscious view would result. That this does not happen brings us back again to our starting point in the word "rakyat" and its failure to continue to be effective. These stories are infused with the assumption of a push toward recognition, as was the case with rakyat. But as in Sukarno's speech, they put off self-consciousness, leaving it for the remote moment when the police show up. They remain outside the realm of the actual, thus in a somewhat spectral world of the *faits divers*, similar to that of the ghosts that the criminals of these stories displaced.

At certain times, however, criminals became more actual (to avoid the word "real"), which, however, scarcely meant that they were appraised at their proper worth. This occurred at moments when the trajectory was thought not to end where it should. At that point, criminals were people such as Kusni Kasdut who have a power independent of the state and who, moreover, call attention to themselves without ever effecting the recognition that would make them an accepted part of the nation. Just then the new criminal type emerged.[7]

4　A New Criminal Type in Jakarta: The Nationalization of Death

One should seek to prevent the regeneration of the body that we bury. Murder only takes the first life of the individual whom we strike down; we should also seek to take his second life, if we are to be even more useful to nature. For nature wants annihilation; it is beyond our capacity to achieve the scale of destruction it desires—de Sade, Juliette, *vol. 4.*

Each sees the other do the same as it does; each does itself what it demands of the other, and therefore also does what it does only in so far as the other does the same. Action by one side only would be useless because what is to happen can only be brought about by both—Hegel, Philosophy of Spirit

Et la haine s'est glissée dans son coeur"—after Racine

"Trauma," not Ghosts

The New Order is marked by the frequency of middle class criminals whose crime is directed against members of the underclass. We have seen some examples already in the last chapter. Frequently there are reports of the delinquent sons of members of the elite. I want to begin with one such case, the adopted son of a high official. One might think he is rebellious, but in fact, rather than being thought to act against his father, the latter, it is suggested, is somehow implicated in the crime. One might think the news of such criminals would amount to an indictment of the ruling class. But it is the reverse. In the end, there is, if not necessarily harmony, certain connections established between the very high and the very low.

On 28 August 1993, *Pos Kota* had a headline that read "Policeman Killed and Then Burned on a Rubber Estate in Cianjur," Cianjur being a place between Jakarta and Bandung. Above this in smaller bold letters was: "Kidnapped from a Police Post by Plotters with Motor Vehicles." Villagers discovered a burning body and, putting out the fire, found it to be that of a police agent. The story as it eventually unfolded is that two cars drove up to a police post in East Jakarta and requested help, asking Sergeant Bambang Sumartono to follow them. Once at the house of IA, one of the criminals, IA had a servant bring them coffee and then tried to get Sergeant Bambang's pistol. There was a struggle in which IA stabbed the sergeant seven times, killing him, then put his body in the trunk, had the servant clean up the blood, and went in a new red sedan to the village where they burned the body. The headline of an early story features the sedan, which was noted for the strangeness of a new car in that area, and which elicited stories of mysterious new cars circling the area previously. Cars are minor players in the story, much attention being devoted to the blood stains in the trunk, which the servant later confessed to the police he had to wipe up.

By the first of September, the criminals had been caught. There were three of them and they were a type that *Pos Kota* takes pleasure in, namely university students, here called *oknum mahasiswa*. Oknum can only be partially translated into English as "certain students" or perhaps "student types"; it indicates that these students were not acting as students ought to act. *Pos Kota* enjoys showing the corruption of the privileged classes, particularly their children. Since, as I have already noted, this is a scandal preferred as well by the middle class press, it does not indicate much about the political stance of *Pos Kota*. When the story unfolds, *Pos Kota* reports that the motive for the killing was unclear. What is certain is that IA, the ringleader of the three, wanted a pistol. *Pos Kota* at some points makes this seem merely a perverse desire distinguishing it from the uses they might put it to. "The penis and some of the fingers of the corpse were destroyed by the fire" ("Bagian alat vital dan sebagian jari mayat sudah sempat dimakan api.") they report on the second day of their accounts.[1] Later, they confirm that the policeman had been castrated before the body was burned, placing these criminals among the *sadis*.

When they are identified the criminals turn out to be the sons of prominent people.[2] IA, the ringleader, is first noted as the son of a real estate developer. This is dropped without further mention when they learn that he is the adopted son of someone on the supreme court. His mother is never mentioned. Many later accounts focus on the fact that the father, who is wanted by the police for questioning, never shows up at the police station. We have then not only the presumed guilt of a middle class son, but the implication that his father had something to do with it. This implication is reinforced when a criminologist interviewed by the paper asserts that in addition to the three activists, there was "a nonplaying captain," identity unspecified. Another report says that when the car of the criminals drove up to the police station, an unidentified woman pointed repeatedly toward the unfortunate soon-to-be-victim. That is, suspicion spreads but these stories are begun only to be dropped. They implicate not only members of the middle class but also officers of the state. For instance, it is reported that a police agent sold IA hundreds of bullets, which were discovered in the house of the judge along with the pistol.

One asks, "Who is the victim?" *Pos Kota* uses the abbreviation that designates his rank, Serka (Chief Sergeant), in referring to him, at least initially. When they give his biography they cite his place of birth but not the names of his parents, his siblings, his wife, or his children. His biography consists of his civil service number, 5708021, and the record of his career in the police. To *Pos Kota* he was nothing but a policeman. His wife is treated a little differently. She lives in the complex reserved for families of police and she is comforted by her neighbors, all of them from police families. But her siblings come to visit her from her natal village, and we see that she is a villager not so different from those in the place where her husband's body was burned. These relatives are surprised by the large number of visitors who arrive even from other police residential units. The crime is committed against a police agent and it is the police, their families, and villagers who share the widow's suffering.

So we have a crime against the police committed by someone who, given his social position, seems unlikely to have an animus against them. As *Pos Kota* presents it, and it presents it obliquely, the crime was directed at the power of the police, hence the castration. And it was for the purpose of using that power outside the law, hence the policeman's pistol used against him. The criminal, adopted son of a supreme court justice, is, genealogically speaking, a representative of the law. But, given his crime and the implication of his father, he is an illegitimate representative of the law. It is not much different from the policeman himself committing a crime, using his state-owned pistol for private and criminal purposes. Except that the policeman is merely a sergeant and lives in the police barracks whereas IA is from the highest strata of Jakartan society.

Pos Kota does not report much about his motive. But speculation about it, no matter what the particular reasons for the crime tends in the same direction. It implicates the upper classes. Thus the sadis, *Pos Kota*'s term, of IA shows a certain wildness and shocking unpredictability often found in reports of the sons of the upper class. Sometimes the lack of a rational motive, it is suggested, means that other people were involved. There is the "nonplaying captain" and the mysterious woman who points toward the victim. It is evident that *Pos Kota* does not print all it knows. Not having been in Jakarta at the time of the killing, I have not heard any rumors, although I am sure there were some.[3] *Pos Kota* simply hints at the involvement of high authority, but there are many such hints and they are as strong as a Jakarta paper would be allowed to print.

This double attitude is displayed about the police themselves. At the start, *Pos Kota* prominently features the story of some police who sold ammunition to IA. Later the story is scaled down to just one person. But the paper gives the police credit for solving the murder and for capturing the criminals when in fact, or at least according to the paper's own reports, the criminals turned themselves in and confessed at a time when the police were following false leads. The paper, however, goes to great lengths to show how people rely on the police. They quote villagers from the place where the body was found, for instance:

> A resident told how fear had come over nearly everyone in Pasar Angin. "They are daring enough to torture and even kill the police. They wouldn't hesitate with ignorant people like us." (31 August 1993)

We could rephrase the statement this way: "The police are the ultimate or near ultimate barrier against aggression and they themselves have been attacked. Therefore 'we' are not safe." The more the sons of the upper class are wild, violent, and destructive, the more the upper class as a whole, including their agent, the police, is corrupt, the more the police and the state as a whole are necessary. This is not an absolutely original logic and it clearly is not impeccable. But it is altogether common in Jakarta; I never heard anyone complain that it was contradictory or incoherent.

In thinking of this logic, one has to notice how the victims of the criminals have shifted. It is not merely the police who have been aggressed; it is also innocent villagers. One such has appeared in the quotation I just gave you. For this conservative logic to be persuasive, one has to appreciate the particular vulnerability of this class of victims. They are not merely innocent, so were the others. And they were not merely unintended victims; they were also without the defenses that traditionally would have been available to them. To take the first point first, the killing had nothing to do with the spot where the body was found, the location being chosen precisely for its lack of connection with the killing and the victim. The murderers wanted nothing to do with the villagers. Their aim was either the capture of a pistol or the practice of sadism against the police or both. Even if there were a further motive, it did not concern the villagers. Villagers need the police because they cannot themselves guard against a danger they not only cannot anticipate but also cannot fathom. They stand guard for the five days between the discovery of the murder and the arrest of the criminals, fearing for some reason that these criminals will return.

After the capture of the criminals, villagers talk of their fear. One says that now they are relieved (*lega*) and grateful (*berterima kasih*) to the police. Their anxiousness (*kecemasan*) is gone. One tells a reporter this:

> According to Apip, they were not afraid of ghosts (hal-hal gaib) though he had to admit that there were some who felt that way too. "We were very worried, afraid that we would be the target of these people who were wandering around out there for five days." (2 September 1993)

They are not afraid of ghosts, which is to say a lot. That is, it is not the spirit of the murdered policeman or spirits connected with the murderers who might bother them. This is not a relief but a difficulty. The traditional locus of danger does not apply here. If it did, they could rely on traditional remedies, such as amulets and magical or religious experts. But what they fear here is something different. Their fear is reflected in the nature of the illness of those most affected, for instance, the man who discovered the body and put out the fire named Utom:

> According to Utom, from the moment he was putting out the fire with water, his stomach was upset and he felt nervous. He continued to put out the fire even though he kept vomiting. But he kept going until the fire was out (3 September 1993).

The report goes on to say that the body had been soaked in ten cans of gasoline and that it needed a lot of water to extinguish it. No one else would help him. Now he is ill and he can't afford to go to the local clinic or to a doctor. He has a name for his sickness: "He said he was traumatized by this very disturbing event" (3 September 1993).[4] It is not his effort or the effects of fire that made him ill, it is the "very disturbing event." His illness is not fully described by its physical symptoms. It is trauma, the western word, that he uses. Here the word seems to mean that the symptoms cannot be accounted for by physical causes and that the effects are more than physiological. Trauma in that sense is similar to ghostly possession. But it is made explicit that the illness is not caused by ghosts. It is caused by something having to do with this new sort of criminal or something to do with the burning of a policeman's body. Another villager, Enoh, "who had the opportunity to witness it also fell ill" (3 September 1993). Simply seeing it, witnessing it, causes illness. We must ask what "it" refers to here. What is there so particularly disturbing about the event; why does it not produce ghosts who are also associated with death; why is the effect described by the Western word, trauma, while ghosts are explicitly excluded as the source of fear?

A partial answer comes when we think about the fear that the criminals will return. That the villagers fear a return suggests the behavior of ghosts who reappear at the site of death. Apip says that they are not afraid of ghosts, they are afraid of the criminals. But the criminals are like ghosts not only in the way they are thought to haunt the scene of burning but also because they inhabit special sites inaccessible to those who are visited by them. Ghosts, one knows, lurk at the site of death; these criminals "roam around out there" (*berkeliaran di luar'*). The difference between their locus and the usual haunts of the criminals is the difficulty. Villagers could guard themselves, and do, against the sort of local criminals, thieves in particular, who come from places they know about. They can guard themselves against ghosts whose locales they can divine. But the origins of this new sort of criminal are hazy to them.

Pos Kota carried this strange report about the choice of a place to dispose of the body:

> The location chosen shows a new 'modus' because up till now in every murder in Jakarta where the body has been disposed of in Cianjur the corpse was thrown out on the edge of the Jakarta-Bandung road. This time it was 18 kilometers from the Jakarta-Bandung road. (29 August 1993)

The paper uses the word "modus"; it puts the murderers in a special class, the category criminals, those who break the law according to certain methods with which the police are familiar. These criminals, however, are innovators. The policeman was stabbed to death in the house of the murderer. The body was transported quite some distance from there in order to be able to burn it and to dissociate it from the murderers. The village was chosen because it had nothing to do with criminals or with this particular policeman and perhaps because it was outside the usual pattern for the disposal of corpses from Jakarta. The villagers could not anticipate the danger. They were victims of the murderers, victims of "trauma," for a reason that one has to label, "no particular reason." *Pos Kota*'s suggestion is that these murderers are different from the usual, known type of criminal as that category is known to the police. In relation to the murderers, the villagers are not exactly villagers, people who live in a certain way in a certain place and have a delimited set of relationships, in short, a certain identity. They were just anyone at all, anyone who did not know the murderers, and who were outside the circle of people who matter, or even know people who know someone who matters. To the murderers, the villagers were anonymous, without the names necessary to set them in the circuit of people who could lead back to the murderers.

The "shock," which is the other word besides "trauma" used to describe their state, is first caused by the strangeness of the crime. But its effects continue after the crime is solved. No understanding of the crime could account for its effects on them because the story has nothing to do with them. Nothing in their identities could account for why they had to suffer. By the same token, the murderers are without a known place from the perspective of these victims. The murderers come from Jakarta, but Jakarta, or rather the criminals' Jakarta, is a place to which the villagers have no access. Unlike ghosts, who usually have some sort of story to account for their appearances in a particular place, no story, not even one that accurately described the murderers' motivation, could account for why they came, as *Pos Kota* reported, from a discotheque to the police station, to a wealthy Jakarta neighborhood, and finally to the place where they burned the body. Murder alone is not enough to create a new effect, "trauma." Murder has been known for a long time without "trauma." "Trauma" and "shock" are words from the vocabulary of the middle class. They are brought into the village not only with a violent event, but with violence that originates where "trauma," the word, originates in the Indonesian scene. "Trauma" and "shock" come with the intrusion of the ruling class as it makes itself felt to the under class, not merely in the event itself, but through the reporting of *Pos Kota*. The place that one knows one does not know about and cannot fathom used to be the abode of ghosts. Now, in this report of *Pos Kota*, it is the discotheque, the university, the places where youth smoke ganja, and the walled houses of the wealthy.

It is crime that brings the under-class readers of *Pos Kota* into the upper-class world. It is the beginning of communication between these worlds. The newspaper that reports and even produces their story is thus a medium between cultural realms. It produces a story that links classes, one that makes the very choice of the villagers as secondary victims of members of the upper class reasonable. Reasonable, that is, in terms of class and reasonable in terms of modern communications. By the end of the story, the "traumatized" villagers turn from those entirely outside the story into those being sought out.

The transformation of the narrative into one that shows the paternalistic nature of class relations is revealed in the role of the police. The police not only are given credit for catching the criminals, they also assuage the fear of the villagers. A large group of policemen go to the village to pray for their dead colleague and at the same time to thank the villagers who helped by recovering the body while it was still recognizable.

The police made an effort to put the soul of their comrade at rest and, at the same time, to still the effects of the murder on villagers. It is an act of mourning, putting the murder behind the villagers and reestablishing the police not merely as catchers of criminals and protectors of the peace, but as religious figures who reassure. Utom, forty-eight, is said to be *tengah mengalami shock* (continuing to suffer shock), and was earlier said to be unable to afford to go to a clinic or see a doctor. The police doctor comes with the group, however, and tells him, "Stop worrying. We'll take care of everything. It's all in the hands of the police now" (tidak usah terlalu pikirkan kejadian itu, Pak, semuanya sudah ditangani polisi). I am unable to reproduce in English the paternalistic, reassuring, and still dismissive tonality of this policeman. But the sentence means the sick man should stop thinking about the event because it is now in the hands of the police, who are certainly competent to cure his worries. The peasant tells the reporter that he never expected his efforts to put out the fire would take such a toll on him. The police give him a trophy. They also congratulate another villager who helped extinguish the fire and they contribute Rp100,000 for the costs of the ceremony they attend. If relations between the classes are begun, it is because of *Pos Kota*, which makes actualities into typical events. If relations between the classes are also made harmonious, it is because *Pos Kota* shows the police functioning not as catchers of criminals; they are, rather, assuagers of "trauma," if such is possible, and recognizers of civic actions.

The magnification of stories of this sort can be seen by comparison with other sorts of crime stories that appear sometimes in *Pos Kota* and that are, I am certain, much more common in practice. Crimes such as robbery for instance. If one is robbed in Jakarta, one can often get back what one has lost. Thieves are usually members of bands. People know who they are. Police cooperate with them. One need only follow the lines of people who know people to get to the point where one is in communication with them. There are none of the anonymous messages one sees addressed to the New York thief: "No Radio." It is a question of personal knowledge and that is ultimately based on a pattern of kinship. We have already discussed the assumption of this type of communication in speaking of the murder of

Asharudin. This trajectory, however, is feared to be broken down; that is, the fear of the creators of these stories is that there are in fact people outside the channels of communication that run between classes. This is a reasonable fear given the end of the populism of the Sukarno epoch. The remedy is mass forms of communication and stories such as ours where communication is initiated from above. But we are a little ahead of ourselves.

Criminals, upper-class criminals, are turned into something that resemble ghosts. Ghosts are connected with death and death is the subject of the story. The criminals brought a corpse to the village, so death becomes the subject of the upper-class invasion of the peasant world and the occasion for reconciliation of classes. Death in the world of West Javanese rubber tappers would invariably bring to mind ghosts. Here ghosts are denied and criminals take their place. The substitution is perhaps possible because of similarities between the two. Ghosts always want one thing, whatever else they might demand. They want to show up, to appear or to be present, restoring themselves in an impossible way to their condition in life. Which is to say that they remain ghosts because they can never be fully present again. They are always both there and not there at the same time. For ghosts, living persons are the means they need to register their appearance. Most ghosts, or at least Javanese ghosts, have no animus against particular living persons. Those they haunt are haunted only because of coincidence. They have somehow intersected, quite unintentionally, the places ghosts haunt. The villagers in this story come across the criminals only by accident. These criminals, being murderers, bring death with them in the form of the corpse. They are unlike ghosts because, among other things, they are mobile, traveling between places rather than haunting particular sites in the manner of specters. But there are enough resemblances that it would be natural to think of ghosts, and natural enough for a villager, reportedly, to have spontaneously denied that ghosts are involved.

This case is difficult to define because ghosts do not show up and it is asserted that they will not appear and yet this furnishes no relief. Apip says that " 'they were not afraid of ghosts [hal-hal gaib] though he had to admit that there were some who felt that way too,' " but that nonetheless they "were very worried, afraid that we would be the target of these people who were wandering around out there for five days" (2 September 1993). Put into the context of the fears raised by the murder of a policeman: "They are daring enough to torture and even kill the police. They wouldn't hesitate with ignorant people like us." The implication is that these villagers would be grateful if they could believe in ghosts again. Then they would not have to be so afraid; they know what to do about ghosts. The criminals roam around out there, like ghosts, while the villagers have lost their protection against them. The policeman's corpse dumped in their village raises fears that they cannot name. If they reject the fear of ghosts at this moment it is, of course, because national authority has already been assimilated into their mentality. To some degree at least national authority has already replaced traditional protection against harm, but the murder shows that it cannot be relied upon.

These villagers do not know precisely what they fear. They themselves suffered no material damage by the arrival of the corpse in their midst. But they did suffer the effects of fears raised as they put out the fire. These effects, their "trauma," are understood in *Pos Kota* by reference to the sadis quality of the murderers. IA and his friends castrated the policeman and took his pistol. Sadis is not only demonstrated by the monstrosity of the crime, it is also, I believe, confounded with the gun and the penis as the symbols of power the criminals now control. Just as the corpse of the policeman intervening in the village shows that the police in general can no longer be relied on to protect villagers, so, too, the possession of the gun and the penis of the police indicate that the power of the police has been transferred into the control of criminals. There is a conflation of criminal menace and state power, as though they are a single metaphysical entity.

One might be afraid of criminals when one thinks the police are no longer available. But this does not yet explain why the policeman's burning corpse was thought to produce "trauma." One needs as well to see that the power of the police and the power of criminals were already beyond anything understandable by recounting specific acts. This merely pushes the problem back. How is it that such beliefs arise? It is through the conviction that the power of ghosts is limited and that beyond them there is something that takes their place. Here it is the police or the state and criminals. Rather than asking why it is that ghosts are expected not to appear, it might be better to point out that police and criminals both arise precisely where ghosts were expected before. There would be no "trauma," no inexplicable effects, if full belief in ghosts still existed.

Because ghosts on Java are connected with death we come back to the corpse. The inexplicable effects were transmitted by the burning corpse. The corpse normally would be treated religiously, alleviating fears that arise with death. Here, however, to begin with the corpse is associated with the power of police and criminals. *Pos Kota* draws connections between its effects and castration and stolen guns that make reasonable the fear that criminals still "roam around out there." Nothing can alleviate this fear at first because the villagers had nothing to do with the world of the police and criminals of this type; therefore they were victims. But the helplessness of villagers also was caused by the displacement of thinking about death brought about precisely by ideas of criminal and police power. Death as understood in Sundanese thinking (Sunda being the province of Java where the body was found) might very well account for a fatal accident of some sort. But the usual assurances that life and death are in the control of God, not humans, is of less use when the corpse seems to funnel another sort of supernatural power into the village. These beliefs charge the corpse.

But no ghost is expected. The corpse has become merely an effect of criminals. When no ghosts arise after death, death has not been secularized or reduced to a question of biology or physiology. The usual aftereffects of death, the fear of recurrence, are left unaccounted for. The criminals who "roam around out there" are not the equivalent of ghosts. Ghosts account for the intrusion of death into life. Associated with coincidence, they give a place to chance, making it an expectable part of life and thus no longer chance in the strong sense of that term. The policeman's corpse, its connection with another sort of supernatural being, displace this understanding of death and chance without assuaging the fear that arises with it.

The police, it is evident, were thought to hold off almost every imaginable terror. One can say ghosts do the same. One knows that whatever catastrophe they mark, it is limited to the particular events with which each ghost is connected. Serka Bambang's burning body lifted the barrier against terror. It is by reference to that other barrier, ghosts, that one sees the abyss of fear. Ghosts, which exist, will not show up. In their absence, there are only the stories of *Pos Kota*. And these stories conjure up places and people, which, heard about, are not only outside the experience of readers, but also without coherence. It is precisely because in the end there is the corpse and because the corpse will not produce ghosts that other fears arise, expressed through the idiom of criminals, police, guns, and castration. Unlike ghost stories, which are told with amusement and satisfaction, the stories of *Pos Kota* have no assured tonality. The sensationalism of the paper seems to preclude taking the story seriously. But it would always be possible to read it otherwise. In that case, the references would be harder to contain. It is just at that point that the newspaper arrives with words such as "trauma" and "shock." These words, without specific sense, indicate that someone does understand, hence controls death. These people are the police. It is in this way that a route of communication is said to be opened between the upper and lower classes. If it did not happen, the result might be uncontainable terror.

The lack of traditional beliefs surrounding this incident intensifies the interest in death. One indication of this is the attention paid to witnesses. These are not witnesses to the crime but witnesses to the last moments of the policeman. There is, for instance, the testimony of the sergeant's colleague at the post when the kidnappers arrived. They summoned the sergeant to follow them, alleging some troubles at home.

> "His motorcycle wouldn't start, but finally the engine caught and Bambang followed the two cars," Rumini stated.
>
> That was the final exit of the member of the police with the strong body and thick mustache. Because the next day Master Sergeant Bambang Sumarno was come across with his body burned in the rubber grove in Pedaja Village, Cikalong Kulon, Cianjur. (*Pos Kota*, 28 August 1993)

In this mingling of the metaphorical and the factual, disappearance from view is equated with dying. But Serkap Bambang disappears only to reappear again, this time as a corpse. *Pos Kota* insists on a purely visual connection to the deceased again when it interviews the widow after the criminals have been caught. In their issue of September 5th, they show the widow in the same way they have in each of the three pictures of her. She stares into space, focusing on nothing around her, or she looks at the ground, perhaps even having her eyes closed. These are signs of her grief; her mind is numbed and her thoughts are doubtless with her late husband. When she speaks, she says that she wants to see. The headline of the article reads "Even Though Bitter, No Vengeance: Mrs. Herlin Wants to See the Face of Her Husband's Killer." It reads in part:

> Mrs. Herlin Widrastuti expressed her desire to see directly the faces of the three student-types who are accused of killing her husband, Master Sergeant Bambang Sumarno. "Let me be at peace. Even though bitter, I will not seek vengeance," she said with a peaceful expression on her face.
>
> I want to know the one called IA, the step son of the high official of the Supreme Court, said Mrs. Herlin Widrastuti.

In an earlier report she had called for the severest punishment of the criminals. Here she says nothing of the sort. Later, she will repeat that she does not want vengeance and trusts the police to act appropriately. She only wants to see the murderers. She uses the word *lihat,* see, for what she wants. She also says she wants to know (*tahu*) IA. Indonesian has two words that are translated as know in English, *kenal* and *tahu*. One means "be acquainted with" and is the word usually used when speaking of persons. The other simply means to "recognize" or to "register." It is the latter term that Mrs. Herlin Widrastuti uses. She does not want to know IA as a person, which could mean wanting revenge. She disregards him as a person, leaving him to the authorities. But for her peace of mind, she wants to see him. In other words, she wants to see him without knowing him, to see him without trying to see behind his face into his thoughts, motives, or feelings.

Mrs. Widrastuti puts a face on the criminal, as it were. One could imagine that to put a face on the criminal would be to identify him, to make him an image of criminality, or to create a picture of an undesirable other. But this does not seem to be the logic of this widow. To see him without knowing him is to disregard his criminality in favor of his connection with her deceased husband. IA is the best example of the witness to the disappearance and therefore remains connected to her husband. Through him, Mrs. Widrastuti has a link to her husband. It is, of course, not the memory of him as he was when alive. Mediated as it is through the face of the murder, it has something to do with his death.

The criminal here has a special connection with death. IA saw what Mrs. Widrastuti did not, her husband at the moment he died. IA for Mrs. Widrastuti is like a camera that can preserve something for someone not present when the picture was taken. Roland Barthes says of a photograph taken in 1865 of a prisoner about to be executed for his attempt to assassinate the U.S. Secretary of State that he dies two deaths: one historically, soon after the photograph was made, and a second time as he is recreated again in his picture, with Barthes present. IA, the murderer, is also the preserver not merely of her husband's last moment alive, but also of him past that moment, as though he could live again in the way the prisoner did for Barthes, which is to say in a register where he is at once dead and alive. Mrs. Widrastuti no longer concerns herself about the murderous deed of IA. Instead of breaking her link with her husband, IA preserves it and, it seems, preserves it after death. This criminal makes the dead reappear and in that sense he produces in himself an equivalent of the villagers' missing ghost.

But class matters quite a lot. IA's Mrs. Widrastuti is characterized as a villager who remains in her affinities a villager. From her statements, she appears to be a person much like the villagers who found her husband's burning body. In the end, IA, the adopted son of a supreme court justice shows how the upper class controls death. It may well be, and it is even likely, that low class murderers, too, could have the same ability to stand between the living and the dead. But if so, they not only do not link classes, they threaten whatever stability exists between them. They also challenge the myth being forged out of violence in the pages of the press. As it stands, IA is the living embodiment of the man he killed. From this report, he has absorbed Serkap Bambang and so, like the police who cure "trauma," he has assuaged grief and shown the bond between supreme court justices, their high-living university student sons, and helpless villagers. The murderer himself, then, is the best witness not to the crime but to his victim, putting him to death but keeping him present. It is this new form of ghost that villagers feared.

This upper-class criminal, embodying his victim, intruding on other low-class victims, links upper and lower classes, reestablishing the bond between them, which eroded in the course of the New Order. That the bond passes through "death" and "trauma," redefining the first and introducing the second, is an effect of nationalization, "death" being no longer what it was in Sundanese or other regional worlds; it is instead defined in terms of Indonesia, national ties of the sort technologically possible in Suharto's regime being added to local ones.[5]

More "Trauma," Another New Criminal

The upper-class criminal may tie classes together. But his urge to violence has to be thought of separately from his social function. I do not want to reconcile these facts; they merely exist side by side, or at least have done so in the New Order up until the moment at which I write this sentence.

The intrusion of the ruling classes on the lives of the underclass took a flagrant turn in 1983 and early 1984 when headlines like this one appeared:

> Flat on His Face in the Gutter Covered With Stones a Man Tattooed with a Picture of a Naked Woman Found Dead Stabbed 100 Times (*Pos Kota*, 3 January 1984)

Though this is the major story on the page, and though *Pos Kota*'s report is usually lengthy, this time there was only one sentence:

> A Man with a Tattoo of a Naked Woman, Abdul Kadir alias Oding (21) was found dead, killed, with 100 stab wounds, in a gutter, the drain in front of the houses at Rt 0012/07, Kp. Duku, Kalurahan Kebayoran Lama, Monday morning.

There is apparently no need to say more. By that time people had been finding bodies of tattooed men in most places in Indonesia; they were reported in the press nearly every day. These killings were labeled "Petrus," a neologism made up of two words, *penembak* ("shooter") and *misterius* ("mysterious"). They were not a mystery for long. The government, though it first denied its involvement, soon acknowledged itself as the perpetrator. The victims were known as *gali*, itself an acronym for "the savage class." Gali were for the most part petty criminals, members of gangs. Many of them had worked for the government party, GOLKAR, during the elections the previous year, then were discharged to go back to their old ways. Most gali bore tattoos.[6]

One after the other headlines announced the lurid:

> Blood soaked corpse found in Senayan (a region of Jakarta) 3 Men Murdered, Their Necks Snared with Plastic Rope (*Pos Kota*, 12 September 1983)

The man who found the body, "terrified, ran to the nearest police post panting out of breath reported what he had seen." There is a graphic description of the condition of the corpse.

Pos Kota's stories featured little besides the descriptions of corpses, the finding of them, and the way in which the news was reported to the police. In contrast *Tempo* had elaborate features on the subject. In the issue of 16 April 1983 there was an article with the headline "Hunting Down Gali in Yogya" "Berburu Gali di Yogya" (54). The subtitle says what it is about:

> Store owners in Yogya are frequently subject to extortion. Ninik died after being tortured by purse snatchers. The garrison then took tough steps: five *gali* were shot dead. Some asked legal aid from the LBH [Legal Aid Institute].

The article reports that many in Yogya were quite happy with these steps and made a comparison with 1965 when presumed members of the Indonesian Communist Party were massacred:

> Frankly, the people of Yogya feel grateful for the steps the garrison has taken. "In short, wipe them out, like the PKI (Communist Party of Indonesia) once before," Junaidi hopes.

Junaidi is not identified. Others complained it was not fair; only some gali were shot or arrested and not others. The army commander, Lt. Kol. M. Hasbi, who led the operation in Jogjakarta, said he wanted to assure there would be no disturbances in June of that year when there was to be a total eclipse of the sun and there would be foreign visitors.

> If foreign guests are bothered, they will say, "Don't go to Indonesia. There are lots of pickpockets, robbers, . . ." And we will be the losers. In fact, right now tourists are treated with impudence.

But it was not just to protect the tourist trade that the military commander took over the duties of the police whom, he claimed, were unable to handle the situation.

> They are not so plain as you might think. The leaders of the gangs can take in Rp1 million a month. Think of it! . . . And these *gali* have close connections with one another. Lots of *gali* from Semarang and Surakarta come to the funerals when their friends in Yogya are shot dead.

What he objects to are three things: that these gangs are sadis as mentioned in a previous quotation, that they are organized, and that they take in a great deal of money. And one should not forget his first concern: that Indonesia will be made known to the world as the site of criminals.

This justifies shooting them:

> Why shoot them? Basically we want to act in a humane way. But they resist. We want them to identify themselves. I take full responsibility before the Almighty God for these steps. . . . They think, why should I became a welder, an electrician or another laborer of some sort when as a gali, just from one store, I can get Rp5000 a day.

From this statement and others it is evident that the gali are small time criminals. It is true that they operate in bands, (something one never learns from *Pos Kota*), but to compare these with the mafia makes sense only if one then asks who the heads of the mafia are and their connections with the government, something that does not emerge from these reports. The concern here is with something else. *Tempo,* for instance, reports on one of these bosses. He controlled a casino in Jogjakarta. It is impressed not with the extent of his operations, but with how much he earns and what he does with it. This gali is described as a good father and a husband who provides for his family generously.

> His house in Kampung Jlagran (sic) is grouped with the very best (paling bagus): ceramic floor tiles, thick roof tiles. A stereo set. It has a big carved bed, Jepara style. And he is capable of building an even bigger house in a "more fitting" neighborhood. That is the life style of

> Supeno, the life style of someone called gali or *preman* or *centeng*, who seems to control several parts of the city and surroundings of Jogja" ("Gaya Supeno, Gaya Hidup Gali Yogya. *Tempo*, 30 April 1983: 51)

These criminals want what everyone finds desirable. Unlike the soldier who fell in love with a woman a few years older than his wife, they have no special desires. What we want, they want. The subtitle of this piece reads:

> What's called gali or preman are asked to turn themselves in. If it is necessary they will be hunted down and shot. A preman can take in Rp1.5 million a month—and have a house and furnishings like those of someone with a big income.

They are extremists, but there should be nothing wrong with that if they only want what is proper. The difficulty is, of course, that they do not earn their money properly. The result is that people who would otherwise be laborers live like the legitimately wealthy and become practically indistinguishable from them.

The word that *Tempo* often uses to describe luxurious houses is "top" from the English. This word refers particularly to the expensive and often the foreign. Adolescents who go to top discotheques find them in the hotels that cater to foreigners. *Tempo* from time to time runs articles about these adolescents, who often get into trouble with the police. They are the children of Jakarta's establishment. The high spending of these children is a cause for worry. This is for several reasons, the uncertain origins of the money being one of them. But the worry is expressed as a doubt about character as corrupted by wealth.

Top, in other words, is ambiguous. It is at once what everyone should aspire to, and it indicates something unwanted in those who can afford it. The question of the gali makes this ambiguity explicit. Those who should be workers earn too much. They have what we all want and some presumably deserve. Between the deserving and others there is no distinction apparent. It is a version of the palsu, but this time it is no longer implicitly admired but, rather, feared. In the figures of these tattooed gali one finds combined a version of the palsu, a source of violence, and an uncontrolled force of expression that reaches even beyond Indonesia's borders. Violence, power of expression, and the ability to counterfeit are given a single source.

President Suharto saw these gali as incarnations of inhuman cruelty who created a generalized and destabilizing fear. Here is a passage from the first edition of his *Autobiography*. (It has been excised from later editions):

> The real problem is that these events (Petrus) were proceed by fear and nervousness among the people (rakyat). Threats from the criminals (jahat), robberies, murder and so on all happened. Stability was shaken. It was as though the country no longer had any stability. There was only fear. Criminals (jahat) went beyond human limits. They not only broke the law, but they stepped beyond the limits of humanity. For instance, old people were first robbed of whatever they had and then killed. Isn't that inhumane? If you are going to take something, sure, take it, but then don't murder. Then there were women whose wealth was stolen and other peoples' wives even raped by these criminals and in front of their husbands yet. Isn't that going too far? Doesn't that demand action? (364)[7]

President Suharto fears that criminals upset the stability of the country. He does not stress the amount of their crimes but their extraordinary violence. They "stepped beyond the limits of humanity." His reference, though he did not use the word, was to the sadis. But the reports of sadis in great measure concerned not the sort of criminals who comprised the gali, but rather middle class bosses who raped their servants or fathers who slept with their daughters. Sadis in the press was at least as much a middle class phenomenon as it was a trait of these small scale criminals. The fear expressed by Lt. Kol. M. Hasbi was that one had turned into the other. Behind the normal and established lurked savagery.

For President Suharto there was, before he began Petrus, "only fear." He claims his own actions were taken to eliminate that dread. And yet his method was to create more of the same. The army, he says, shot only when necessary: "they" are sadis, "we" are not. But the reports in the papers give a different picture. We have seen one from *Pos Kota* already; I could furnish perhaps a hundred others. *Tempo* reported on just this aspect in August 1983:

> 10 shots completely tearing open a body apparently is not a record. Dr. Abdul Mun'im Idies, Sekretaris Lembaga Kriminology Universitas Indonesia, recorded a victim of a mysterious shooting (without quotes) found on July 25 on Jagorawi Street with 11 bullet holes and there are even some 'eaten up' by 12 bullets. "We even inspected a corpse that has 5 bullet shells in its head," he stated. ("Ada dor ada ya, ada yang tidak," 6 August 1983: 12–14)

One might speak like Suharto and say, "if you are going to kill, sure, kill, but once is enough." It is a serious comment. Can one kill more than once? What is the point of twenty stab wounds or a dozen bullet holes in a single victim? It is not different in its excessiveness from the manifestations of the sadis. Perhaps it is for display; the display of force and the willingness to use it. In any case, there was already a certain identification between the murderers of Petrus and their victims, if one speaks from the point of view of class. From that perspective, the president's disclaimer is not so much a disavowal of governmental sadis as the opposite. The president continued:

> Doesn't that demand action? Automatically we had to give it the *treatment* (in English), strong measures. And what sort of measures? Sure, with real firmness. But that firmness did not mean shooting, bang! bang! just like that. But those who resisted, sure, like it or not, had to be shot. Because they resisted, they were shot.[8]

In response to the sadis, when the criminals resisted, soldiers shot them. In Suharto's account it sounds like the operations of the law. But the soldiers who shot were disguised, often with their faces covered. Furthermore stories from families of victims do not report resistance. The "firmness" of the government is a display of strength, but a strength derived not from its authority as the law but from another source, one not different from that of the criminals, judging from the state of the corpses. Attributing sadis to the criminals, the government was stimulated to act as they did.

It would have been possible to proceed legally or at least with the appearance of legality in putting down criminals. Confessions of criminals, registered in law courts, would have produced a different effect. Their admissions, false or true, of the atrocities they committed would have simply put them outside the pale of normal society and distinguished them from the government that acts with steady, legal procedures. The government would be seen to act from motives wholly different from those of the criminals. But by multiply wounding these gali and accusing gali of acting in just that way, the government, and President Suharto himself, implicitly identified themselves with their victims even as they asserted their differences from them. It is the imitation of the criminal that is predominant while the assertion of difference at this point was mere camouflage. It is what makes this case different from the African or European examples cited in the introduction. In those, the attempt is to create an Other; here, there is the assertion of identity with the victims. It is an example of murdering those professed to be like oneself.

Difference was asserted through a claim of superior power, a claim that rested on maintaining the profession of identity. The government, as we have repeatedly said, turned gali into corpses intended to indicate not merely the danger of anyone daring to act as they were presumed to act, but also the unlimited power, inherent not merely in the sadistic quality of these criminals but in something beyond it that made it necessary to kill each criminal several times. When it is unrestricted, the power of the government is claimed to be equal to the power of its adversaries. The force of the government was made equivalent to the power attributed to these corpses precisely when the victims were murdered multiple times.

The government's claim rests on showing that such a power exists; that multiple wounds serve a purpose. The way was prepared by the existence of kriminalitas as we have described it with its inherent violence and its always incipient expressiveness. But until the Petrus incidents, this was kept within the boundaries of the faits divers. Something more was necessary for there to be a question of national importance. Suharto claimed that criminals themselves brought this about with the fear they created. But, although there may have been an increase of crime after the national elections as those who had worked for the government turned to illegality, there was nothing like the panic the president described. His statement gives the kriminalitas of the press a status it never enjoyed before the government began displaying the corpses it created. It is a question of how the power attributed to the corpse is made to seem a menace not for a certain set of villagers as in the case of IA but for the nation as a whole.

It is the government's own resort to extralegal violence that gave it this status. This is not a moral or a legal question. It is rather that when the government explicitly abandoned legality in its actions, it did so by claiming the necessity of acting against a force that it posited was otherwise uncontrollable. It acted against a strength that was inhuman. By acting as the criminals they opposed acted, the government claimed to capture this strength for itself. One might say that it tore it out of the grasp of the criminals, as though this power were transferable.

In the faits divers, the force of criminality never fully revealed itself. It only showed its full dimensions through the action of the government. The government gave kriminalitas a nation-wide significance. In retrospect, the power of kriminalitas appeared when the government, acting like criminals, made the implicit explicit. The violence of the government reflected the violence of the criminals. The force of criminals passed into the hands of the government. At that moment kriminalitas appeared to be something more than was already manifest in the specific acts of particular persons. Kriminalitas, Suharto proclaimed, had the power to create a generalized state, "only fear," and that power became a property of the state.

For the government to act like criminals in order to have their power it had first to see in itself the possibility of being like them. The criminals had to mirror the government before the government could mirror the criminals. I can only speculate as to how this happened. One thinks of 1965–1966, at the inception of the New Order when the government instigated a massacre, once again outside legal procedures and once again leaving bodies in public places. In any case, there are those among the middle class who fear that they are not distinguishable from criminals. Moreover, the killings began when some of those who had worked for the government party during the elections, no longer being needed, were discharged. The similarities between murderers and victims are thus multiple. But when President Suharto speaks of their sadis, or inhuman qualities, he makes the criminals unrecognizable. The moment of reflection of one by the other is marked as much by this unrecognizability as it is by the assertion of similarities. Recognition by the government of itself in the form of criminals is thus uncanny.

President Suharto said this about the fact that the corpses were left in the streets and the rivers:

> So the corpses were left where they were, just like that. This was for *shock therapy* [in English]. (364)

"Shock therapy," means to shock in order to cure. This therapy is directed not at criminals, but at the general populace. The corpses were left where they were, he continued,

> So that the crowds (*orang banyak*) would understand that faced with criminals there were still some who would act and would control them.

Practicing this therapy, President Suharto is in the same position as IA and his friends who "traumatized" villagers, and, of course, by the same means, the display of murder victims. Presumably the initial anonymity of the actions, the appearance of masked men at night, the abductions of men from the midst of their families, were part of "shock therapy," little different than terrorizing.

But if there were terror one might expect that people would flee from the sight of the Petrus corpses. The opposite was the case. They became attractions not only to newspaper readers but to people on the streets where the bodies were distributed. The attractive power of corpses—confined, to those known as Petrus corpses—indicates something about them that people, including the president, found fascinating even if it terrorized.

The corpses were made into warnings, a form of sign. One can ask how such signs can be constructed. It is not merely that to be warnings these corpses needed the explanations given in the press. They were more than merely illustrations of what others said. These criminals, of course, were never brought before the courts; they were merely criminals by accusation. Their tattoos were enough to indicate their kriminalitas. They bore a mark that, the state declared, identified them as criminals; they were condemned simply by having incisions on their skin rather than because of specific crimes they were judged to have committed.

In the eyes of the government, the tattoo did not represent what the wearer of the tattoo intended. It spoke beyond any such intention, signaling first that its bearer was targeted. Later it was what distinguished the corpses of gali from other dead bodies. It was the sign of a menace that was not measurable by the history of the person, even if the person concerned was in fact a gali. Had it been otherwise the newspapers would have given the criminal history of the people killed. Instead the tattoo, after death, proclaimed a menace. It indicated that each such bearer had attracted a lethal power, and that this mark had a power of attraction quite apart from any deeds actually committed or any intention of the person. As the statement of President Suharto shows, the attraction of this mark was its indication of a power attributed to 'kriminalitas' greater than the force manifested by the acts of any particular criminal.[9]

Tattoos in the context of the massacre marked the bearer as unrecognizable in his everyday identity. For instance, he was no longer the person who boasted of his sexual prowess through the picture of a naked woman on his chest. He was now someone capable of calling the government to him despite whatever name he bore or whatever family he had, despite his occupation or anything else that might serve to identify him. An ahistorical force thus seemed to manifest itself through this disarticulation of the person from the marks on his body. It was just this force that the government claimed for itself.

The corpses left in the streets keep the moment of disappearance from life vivid, retaining that moment in the present. It is in that way that gali were turned into communiques. "I was murdered," or perhaps, "we murdered him," is the substance of the warning. The dead person was a notice posted to others. He was the essential element of Suharto's "shock therapy." His dead body displayed in public turned him into a messenger for his killers. The corpse was endowed with "death," which means the capacity to transmit "trauma" and to create "shock," quite unlike the corpses of those who died within the world governed by Javanese culture. The Petrus corpses, made into warnings, spoke; but they spoke for the government.

They spoke principally through their tattoos. These marks came to mean that the persons bearing them had in them a supernatural power evidenced by their attraction of death. Their corpses brought the force of "death" as close to the living as they could come. It is this that made them fascinating. This, I posit, is why Mrs. Widrastuti wanted to see the murderer of her husband, the person who had seen her husband last, and who kept him present to her not as a person but as he existed in his last moments alive and just after his death. Seeing the murderer she was close to the force inherent in this new form, "death."

One has to realize that this is partly an effect of seeing at the second degree. For instance, the tattoo, as reported in the press and as shown in photographs, is not the tattoo as it might have been seen on the skin of its bearer. When the tattoos appeared in newspapers, their marks became typical. Rather than indicating that the bearer was a member of a certain gang or that the tattoo was a written form of his name, tattoos came to be seen in the context of the events not merely as a range of meanings but as an expressive force. This is because each of them contained all the expressive power of the entire conglomeration of similar signs. The effect is something like what an amateur might get looking at a set of hieroglyphics, knowing that they said something, but unable to know what in particular.

Likewise the face. The face of IA for Mrs. Widrastuti was the face of an individual. But it also had the force of its genre, that is, the force of the kriminalitas of all the faces appearing each day in Pos Kota. If Mrs. Widrastuti could find a force of "death" looking IA in the face, it was because he was not a person but something that peered out of nearly every square inch of Pos Kota's front page every day. Which is to say that it was not simply for Mrs. Widrastuti, thinking of her dead husband, that IA's visage was significant. It was the same for Pos Kota's readers who were never acquainted with Serkap Bambang and would never see IA in life. In Pos Kota's photographs, the face was detached from its power to express the character of the person and instead came to speak only of a generalized menace.

"Death," unlike biological or Javanese death, had a power of communication necessary to "shock therapy," one that depended on the government's murders. But the construction of "death" also drew on the sense of menace that already existed before the New Order, the menace left precisely by the formation of the nation against the illegitimacy of the prenational family. The half-accomplished revolution meant that new structural forms were not generated that might have become stable symbols of revolutionary success. The inability to institutionalize revolution might be inherent in it. But when the revolution accomplished only the expulsion of the colonists when many wanted radical changes in Indonesian society, one does not need to make such an assumption.

Sukarno's attempts to alleviate this menace through his notion of "the people" and his formulations of "the revolution" remained incomplete in his lifetime. They were, nonetheless, more efficacious than anything in the Suharto regime, during which the state grew apart from the rest of the nation.[10] The result was an increment in the amorphous sensation of menace. The tattooed corpses of the 1983–1984 massacre were only the strongest expression of this threat. The expressive force at once generated and left unsatisfied with the formation of the nation and the revolution precipitated several effects during the New Order. Among them was widespread counterfeiting, which has within it a certain creativity linked to the market. But for the most part it left a lingering sense of peril, usually pushed into the insignificance of faits divers.

The sense of menace that collected around kriminalitas still remains. For this fear to move outside the boundaries of faits divers and take on national dimensions it needed the initiative of the government. Structurally speaking it needed the corpse like Serkap Bambang's; the corpse before it became a sign. If one can believe the reports, his corpse had a bewildering effect on the villagers who discovered it. It was a sudden intrusion of an unknown, unaccounted-for murder victim into spaces where it could not have been anticipated. The power of the corpse, its capacity to open up references that could not be controlled, is essential to seeing what happened in that case. It is not as "death" in either the national or the local sense that this intrusion took place. It was, rather, from the first the intrusion of death that had no available context. It was death that occurred in a place where the nation was split among classes afraid to be separated from one another and thus lacking common references. It is only on this foundation, if one can use that word, that national "death" was formulated.

There remains the difference of Petrus corpses that attracted attention and the corpse of the police agent that was said to "traumatize" and produce fear without fascination. The attraction of the Petrus corpse was its power, a power considered already restrained, if not completely dominated, once corpses were made into signs. The very presence of the corpse on the street came to mean what the government wanted it to mean. But only on condition that before the corpse spoke for the government it spoke for itself. It had to be seen as having the possibility of creating fear of the sort found in the rubber tappers' village when ghosts will not appear. This alone would make it repugnant. To be attractive its power had to be thought to be under control. Then it could be approached.

The attractive power of the corpse rested on claiming the disruptive power of the corpse. This power was associated with the criminals of kriminalitas and then claimed by the state. The corpse of Serkap Bambang was still active through its effects, not only as long as the murderers were at large, but even after their arrest. So long as no one claimed to have taken that power for himself, "trauma" ensued as the force of the corpse was fused with that of the criminals. The police who returned to the village, claiming everything was in their hands, shifted the balance of assumptions toward control. As the widow wanted to see the murderer, the villagers had to see the police who had achieved control of him and through him of the corpse. The murderer blends into the figure of the police, and, because of his manner of controlling criminality, into the face of President Suharto. Thus government became the therapist of shock therapy.

It leaves the corpse in an ambiguous if not contradictory position. On the one hand, it is the sign of a power that it has as a corpse before it is understood in the context of regional or national death; on the other, that power has passed into the hands of those who murdered but only by being made conceptual. At that moment, its power, which is its ability to displace concepts, is diminished. This unresolved quality of the national corpse indicates that the government never fully possessed its force and never could. There is a paradox in their notion of the power of that dead body such that its force always exceeds the power of murderers. Each corpse came to indicate not the person of the criminal killed but a power associated with death in general and therefore beyond itself. The dead bodies of gali may have demonstrated that the government can control this power but only on the contradictory assumption that leaves this force in a form that is always elsewhere and therefore beyond its control. Had the government full control of its putative force, the power would evaporate or be routinized into the merely human power of government as we know it. The reference of the force of kriminalitas and of the government is never exhausted. However many gali the government killed they could not be sure that they had subdued this supernatural power and taken it for their own. They killed more. The massacre founded itself on a logic in which each murder demanded another. Only in that way could the source of power beyond the state at once be said to exist and to be controlled by it. The nationalization of death is a result of this terrible passage between the state and its citizens.

The question remains why the government did not deal with this menace through its legal institutions. Their very weakness made them available for such a purpose. Indonesian courts are at the disposition of the government. Daniel Lev has remarked that in the history of the country no political trial has ever ended in acquittal.[11] Perhaps it is the weakness of the legal tradition that made show trials an unacceptable response. I cannot fully answer this question except to return to the establishment of the law in Indonesia. Lev has shown how little autonomy there is in the remnants of legal institutions left by the Dutch. But the idea that the Indonesian nation is itself the source of the law, if not exactly all of its legal institutions, is inherent in the relation of family and nation I have described in the first chapter. As the source of morality replacing the ignorance of the prenational family, the nation is the source of the most fundamental law, that governing sexuality. This makes it all the more probable that the government would proceed with the semblance of legal procedure and thus claim the authority of the nation.

That there were massacres instead of legal procedure is due in my estimation to two facts. First, the Indonesian nation may be the source of law, but only through a process that initially must be itself illegal. The law cannot descend from the law; it has to be founded on something outside itself. At the beginning of the nation, it found its initial impetus in the regulation of the family without ever attempting to justify the need to regulate sexuality. Something of this continues when one remembers the interest in incest and adoption we have examined. The law refounds itself in the New Order, if only ambiguously, not against sexuality but against death. The New Order controls death as nationalism originally set itself up as the regulator of sexual morality. The New Order regime's control rests on showing not that it is subject to the law and acts in legally prescribed ways, but on demonstrating that it itself is the source of the law. The New Order was initiated with a grand massacre; it repeats this lethal gesture, giving evidence of its autonomy from anything before it. Simultaneously it deals with the menace left by uncompleted Indonesian nationalism and revolution, a menace it has aggravated. Its reassurance consists in assimilating historical menace to contemporary "death."

The reassurance, such as it is, that terror rests in the control of the government may rebind the state to the nation. However it merely reaffirms the gap between the classes while it suppresses further the expression of the people. One can, therefore, expect more kriminalitas and other forms of expression we have not foreseen. Furthermore, one sees that while kriminalitas exists as a power up for contention, no one can fully possess this power due to the nature of death. Death is nationalized, but, inherent in the narrative structure of repression and by the terms of the massacre it remains always out of reach. It is the misfortune of contemporary Indonesia that "death" has become a lure for those eager to establish their power and their position.

Epilogue: Some Methodological Remarks

There is a difference between the story of Serkap Bambang and that of Petrus. The first account comes only from the newspapers; what I might have found out had I been able to speak with the people involved might have been different. I have claimed only to speak of the formation of a mental framework and, further, one that is imposed, although in my opinion not explicitly, by one class upon another. Perhaps, had I been able to collect the actual reactions to the case, I would see resistance that does not appear in the newspaper. Though I regret not having had the opportunity to go to the rubber tappers' village or to speak with Mrs. Widrastuti, I do not think that this omission is critical. The reason for this has to do with my experience in Indonesia.

As an ethnographer I began by doing fieldwork. When I started to work in Jakarta in 1980, I had already worked extensively in Sumatra and Java, and thought I had refined a method particularly suited to work in cities. When I worked in Central Java using the Javanese language, I decided that whatever the people of the city I met were interested in I would investigate. It was left to me to attune myself to what I heard or overheard and to listen in the first place for tonalities because these were the best clues to finding interest. I followed this method in Jakarta for almost two years. But in the end I was disappointed. It is not that the people I knew in Jakarta (and there were a great range of types and personalities) were without interests. It was, rather, that, unlike Central Java, one interest did not lead to another. In Jakarta I did not find the interconnection of interests that I did in Central Java. There was, instead, a certain disassociation of the person from their interests that meant that no more generally analyzable points emerged. The question that arose for me was why this was the case.

I concluded that it was a difference of languages. In Sumatra and Java I worked within local languages. It was in these languages that people made the associations that I uncovered. In Jakarta I used Indonesian, the national language, at least for the most part. There are many Javanese in Jakarta and I lived in two Javanese households for eighteen months. But the people in these households used Indonesian predominantly. Javanese tended to be almost a private language, used within the family, or sometimes between friends. But when the subject turned to politics, or to religion, or other public questions, the language used was Indonesian. Something happened within Indonesian, a repression of associations that were not recuperated within the discourse of regional languages, or at least the regional languages I knew when spoken in Jakarta. Javanese, when it was used for public questions, was used by the president and others to cite uplifting phrases and correct moral homilies.

In Indonesian, a structure of repression had arisen. I have traced this historically in another book.[12] Here, through the notion of kriminalitas, I have tried to show how public discourse is formed around a certain topic. I was particularly led to this topic because, since 1969, I have been gathering accounts of the massacre of 1965–1966. Initially, in Sumatra, I was able to find executioners and others who were willing, and even eager, to tell me of their activities at the time.[13] But later, when I continued to look for accounts in Java I was struck by the unwillingness of people to talk about the massacre, a response that was duplicated by other researchers who tried to do the same. It is not impossible to find such accounts, but the urge of survivors to vindicate themselves and to preserve their version of events for their successors is notably missing.[14] The problem is to find out why.

My answer is given in this book, and in particular in this chapter. When rubber tappers reportedly do not expect ghosts it does not matter much if this is merely a fabrication of the writers of *Pos Kota,* though I do not believe that it is. Not to expect ghosts is the first step on the path that leads to refinding an equivalent in the state itself. It is a repositioning of fear and reassurance whose effects I witnessed in the lack of production of associations and in the suppression, even by former communists, of their own histories. It is particularly effective because it links the production of fear and its assuagement to the state. One sees in this story a narrative of repression that existed already in Indonesia, but I do not want to blame this repression entirely on the New Order. It seems to me that its roots are in the complicated relation of nationalism and revolution that I traced in the earlier work to which I have already referred. Already in the 1930s for instance, in the popular detective fiction of Sumatra, the detective did not detect; that is, there was no question of conflicting interpretations of the world whose interpreters can demand vindication. The detective in these stories is also the political leader who simply knows the truth, an authority whose position assures his knowledge.[15] The equivalent in the stories of *Pos Kota* is the lack of interest in the trial. When the police arrive to arrest the criminal, the story is over. Alternative versions of events that would be inscribed in justice are ruled out. In this structure, there is no room for contesting interpretations, for the claim to make one's own story prevail; in brief, there is no room for survivors of massacres to tell their own stories.

But this structure is not unshakable. It is vulnerable in its foundation, that is, in its reliance on death and on the corpse. As I have pointed out, just at the moment when death is described, a multiplicity of references are opened up upon which the subsequent structuring of the story depends. This opening of references is essential to the narrative I described. It also reflects the shaken understandings of death that, whether in truth or in fiction, appear in the expectation that ghosts will not appear. It is on that assumption that, with the action of the government in 1983–1984, the finding of corpses, till then merely a subject for faits divers, exceeded that rubric. But, of course, it exceeded it only to find itself reformulated in larger political discourse. From this point of view, fait divers are a repository of fears and their assuagement, available, under certain circumstances, for more general purposes. But the outcome of the story is not always assured.

Kriminalitas is a phenomenon of the New Order, but crime as fait divers is scarcely new to the Indies. Henk Schulte Nordholt and Margreet van Till have pointed out that crime in the colonial society of the turn of the century was often "entertainment."[16] Bandits of that period were the subject of popular theater and popular fiction. (See in particular Pramoedya Ananta Toer ed., *Tempo Doeloe,* Jakarta: Hasta Mitra, 1982). But there was a complicated structure that prevented criminals from becoming anticolonial heros while they were feared by Europeans. In nineteenth-century Java, at the time of the ethical policy, when there was a movement for reform of the colonies, crime was blamed on Chinese and on corrupt officials in league with them. There were also Javanese "bandits" (*jago*), who operated in collusion with officials. With the development of anticolonial sentiment later, one would have expected these bandits to be turned into anticolonial heros. Even though similar types were important in the Indonesian revolution, one cannot say that criminals, reevaluated, were ever enshrined as strugglers against colonialism. Schulte Nordholt and van Till suggest that this did not happen because the Javanese were equally their victims.

But criminals, nonetheless, had a certain caché, an ambiguous status, that one sees in the Jakarta newspapers of today. The difference is that the structure of blindness that leaves criminals out of sight is reproduced differently. The Dutch felt ashamed that there were criminals in "their" Indies. The presence of criminals reflected on them. The Javanese should, according to this point of view, have been protected by colonial officials. The failure of the latter to do so was blamed on their lack of knowledge of Javanese that made criminality undetectable by them. There was, in this view, something to be known about Java and about crime that was hidden. Indonesians did not respond by picking up this possibility of symbolic conflict. I believe this is because of the assumption of lack of communication between Javanese and Dutch. Had they shared a language, perhaps there would have been a different turn.

Given this situation, criminality was left ambiguous. Villagers feared criminals just as the Dutch did; but criminals also were the subject of entertainment. The same is true today. But criminality today is a source of power that is contended for, as we have seen. There is the possibility of strong communication between criminals and others. It is, therefore, not entirely a question of faits divers. It is the changed assumption of communicability, the sharing the national language, that makes this possible.[17] This, of course, is a condition for the massacre of those in one's own image as opposed to foreigners; but it is those "in one's own image" who become unrecognizable. By the same token, given the possibility of communication, one can ask why there is not a stronger demand for justice. Why is it that the story stops with the police? This, I believe, is not merely the propaganda of the state or the upper classes. It indicates the strength of the repression already in place.

5 Counter-Revolution Today: Neither the Story nor Stories—Words and Photographs

Let us compare time to a photographer—earthly time to a photographer who photographs the essence of things. But because of the nature of earthly time and its apparatus, the photographer manages only to register the negative of that essence on his photographic plates. No one can read these plates.
—*Walter Benjamin*

Tempo and *Pos Kota* not only report the finding of Petrus corpses; they also describe public reactions to them. Take, for instance, a report from *Tempo* (6 August 1983). It is in this same account that *Tempo* cites experts speaking of the number of wounds they have found in a single body. They cite a case for its typicality. A body is found floating in a sack in the river:

> People quickly gather on the river bank, in front of the Academy of Navigation near the mosque. Whispering starts to spread: "Its a corpse, a *Petrus* victim."

The police are summoned; they call an organization, Yayasan Palang Hitam, which arranges funerals; a hearse arrives. More people gather, covering their noses, unable to stand the smell (nonetheless they remain there out of unrestrainable curiosity). Traffic is blocked. Finally the sack is opened. "The contents: the body of a pig." . . . "Of course, complaints and curses are hurled. The crowd disperses."

The trajectory—from a source of scandal, to a number of people who talk about it, to the police—is the same as in the cases of domestic scandal. Or almost, since, after the police arrive, still more people come. But in this incident there is no scandal. The reactions do not surprise *Tempo:*

> People these days are obviously *latah* [i.e., they react in an automatic and compelled fashion] when there is a report of a corpse, a myste-

rious shooting victim. Understand: almost every day the papers carry stories—and photos—of victims, their bodies full of holes from multiple bullets. Thrown out.

This scene begins with disgust. One would think the smell and the eventual sight of the corpse would propel motion in the opposite direction. But in these reports it is invariably the contrary. The hope of finding a tattooed, murdered man results in the gathering of a crowd. Here we see the avid, perhaps compulsive interest in the Petrus deaths. According to the journalists, every time a corpse is found a crowd gathers and begins to talk. According to this report, they are forced to talk just as they are forced to come and view something that disgusts them. And it is always the same trajectory: first the need to see and to talk, then the arrival of the police.

Here is the scene described by *Pos Kota:*

> Siblings Are Victims
> 6 Corpses found sprawled out in 3 Places
> Among them, the completely naked. (11 October 1983)

There are two pictures, one showing a large crowd looking down into the water where the corpse is. The report presents it as a multitude of corpses:

> Some floating in the river, some sprawled out on the edge of the road shackled, shot and gashed, some completely naked and some others tied up hand and foot.

In one case the corpse was discovered by Yusuf, an employee of the Jakarta public works department.

> Then word spread from mouth to mouth, until the [water] lock was swarming with people who wanted to see.

There is precision and a self-consciousness about how the news is spread in this report. It is not that a *Pos Kota* reporter saw the news being disseminated. It is, rather, that seeing the crowd, he assumed that it had gathered because "word spread from mouth to mouth." It was not, in his mind, like the crowd that gathers in New York when one person looks up and a couple of dozen do the same. At least not at first. The Indonesian crowd is an effect of rumor. And rumor starts with scandal, while the most compelling scandal is the existence of the "corpse, [the] Petrus victim."

These reports are pictures of the ability of the tattooed dead body to collect interest. That interest is not exactly pious. The effect of the corpse is to attract a diversity of types and reactions, not always compatible with the seriousness of the crime.

> The numbers of people who wanted to see increased all the time. Passing vehicles whose passengers wanted to see what was at the heart of the crowd parked on the side of the street. There were lines and lines of cars, including, indeed, luxurious sedans which stopped as their drivers eagerly looked at this free spectacle.

There is a "free spectacle." In this report it is curiosity that attracts people. At the stage of the report where traffic is blocked, people wanting to see what everyone else is looking at, the corpse might be replaced by another diversion. The corpse formed the first attraction, but by the time the cars stop, it is simply a desire to see whatever might be there to be seen that makes the crowd augment.

This curiosity is corrosive of the purposes of the display. The menace that supposedly comes with the sight of the corpse is vitiated. It is no longer a warning. Entertainment replaces terror. One is perhaps not far from early modern European scenes when hangings were celebrations. Reading certain reports or listening to President Suharto and his army commanders, one should expect a single message and a single tonality. The tangents in other directions are illustrated when someone in the crowd has his pocket picked, just as he might in any other crowd. *Pos Kota* goes into detail:

> The density of the numerous people bumping against each other started mischievous hands working. In the midst of the seriousness [*keseriusan*] of people straining to see the floating corpse, it actually happened that a voice was suddenly heard: "Pickpocket; pickpocket. . . . My wallet was stolen."
>
> The man whose money was taken immediately complained to the police who were busy taking care of the corpse. "Mister, what's going on, eh? My wallet with my driver's license and money is gone. Ah, its really tough!"
>
> Gunawan Setiadi, the man pickpocketed, finally hurried off to report to the police post in Pasar Baru, after being told to do so by the officer mentioned.

What should be a single story, one that has a history, that concerns the "seriousness" (again a word derived from English) of death and the sadis, multiplies into others. The single message of the corpse is replaced with other attractions—fat billfolds among them. The murder of thieves to make sure that theft is kept under control produces more theft. All as a result of uncontrolled curiosity; the gravity of the corpse is turned into the amusement of seeing Gunawan Setiadi interrupt the policeman fishing the body out of the water with a more urgent problem of his own. One has a glimpse of Gunawan's difficulties as he tries to replace his license. The anecdote ends with the police, but the wrong police, Gunawan having lost his way. He has to be pointed to the correct police officer.

The corpse itself, in this instance, proves unsatisfactory. The man was about fifty years old:

> His body was thin and did not yet give off an odor, a sign that it was not long since he died. There was a wound on his temple and blood was still oozing out.
>
> When the corpse was fully visible, it was evident from the faces of the people swarming around that they were a little disappointed. "Sure, its not really a corpse. . . . !" several people grumbled seeing it.

They want to see "death." But what they see is something else; something ordinary. They want to see perhaps more blood, more physical damage. Something more definitive. But apparently the man still looks much as he looked when alive. They never see what they came for; what they were meant to see. "Death" refuses to become apparent. As though one would need to kill the man again, stabbing him twenty times or putting a dozen bullets into him for the corpse to compel the correct tonality in its observers.

If the corpse looked like a corpse, "a Petrus victim," then the *latah* or compelled response (as *Tempo* terms the circulation of information that starts with the discovery of the corpse and ends with the police) would have taken its full course. In its place, there is disappointment and other stories. The crowd does not turn into a collectivity of any sort. It remains a collection of rich and poor, honest and dishonest, each keeping their distinctiveness. Even if the crowd was *latah*, to respond automatically, it would not be "the people," or at least it would not be "the people" as known in the time of Sukarno. Instead of being a group, emblem of the nation, themselves being made known, they are, in these stories, a mere line of communication, running from scandal to authority. Or rather, they are a little more than that because in return they are protected by authority. Authority itself is established as the place where messages terminate.

Petrus and other operations against criminality can be understood as attempts to keep this line of communication operating, to keeping it open as a line that sends one story to one destination. What prevents its proper operation is curiosity, but also the corpse or Petrus victim itself. It should have, ipso facto, a single meaning and evoke a single sensation.

But it did not always, even when the corpse was a mutilated Petrus victim. One cannot be sure that the loss of the billfold is entirely different from the Petrus stories in its origin. Can the urge to take hold of something ever be entirely disengaged from the thought of the loss of life? Here the sight of the corpse stimulates a different and competing trajectory from the typical Mysterious Shooting story.

When the story fails to take its proper path the establishment of authority is no longer the primary issue. One goes to the wrong police; one thinks about other things. The state fades from view. One can imagine other phantasms arising in place. The corpse is not powerless, even when people are disappointed in it. It can produce different stories, some of them about death, some not. One can imagine later, on that site, someone seeing a ghost. This is still common enough in Indonesia and indicates the continuation of older notions.

For President Suharto, Petrus was supposed to ensure that there is only one story, only one source of fiction, and only one ending: the police, the state. For Petrus to be what was intended, "death," meaning the power of the corpse to elicit fear, talk and hope of recourse has to be conjoined to kriminalitas. The sense of an incessant production of kriminalitas, the continuous attempt to make a metaphysical force appear, examples of which we have seen in the last chapters, must be attributed to the Petrus corpse. And the corpse must be killed repeatedly to be thought to have a power that the state then calls its own.

What is at stake in kriminalitas is an uncontrollable origin nonetheless claimed by the state. Against it is the production of the palsu, the stories of incest, and much else that proceeds from no clear source at all.

Photographs and Words

The contribution of President Suharto to Indonesian political culture has been to conjoin the nation and the president in a channel of communication, one that begins with "them," passes through kriminalitas, and ends with him. The nexus criminality-state and nation is vulnerable in the ways we have seen. There is not only the failure of the corpse to produce the right story and the operations of curiosity producing unrelated ones, in the very production of stories there is also something that goes beyond them.

Let us turn back to the murder of Serkap Bambang and look at the photographs. In the issue of September 5 there is a photograph with the caption, "Locus of the Burning of Serka Bambang Visited by East Jakarta Deputy Chief of Police." What it shows is precisely a visit. Five men stand on the edge of the spot where the body was incinerated. They are not actively looking. One might expect to see them close to the ground searching for neglected clues of some sort, in the manner of police detectives, but this is more of a ritual visit. They simply stand and gaze vacantly at a piece of ground, which is distinguishable from the area around it only by being cleared of vegetation. What they are thinking or what the purposes of their visit was is not said in the accompanying report. It is enough that they are simply looking. There is, apparently, nothing much to see. It is a place where something took place, the traces of which have already vanished. It is the sight of a disappearance, the disappearance, nearly, of the sergeant's corpse.

Without the caption one would not be able to make sense of the picture at all. And that, I believe, is the point. Behind what is shown in the photo, not merely out of sight but necessarily invisible, is "death," the realm of "death." When the police gaze at the blank ground, presumably they picture Serkap Bambang there. There, but also out of sight, disappeared, dead. The site, s-i-t-e, is a sort of camera, bringing the absent into mental representation and establishing that he is not there. The site or sight of something no longer present might be unmanageable. One could have any number of thoughts, one could be terrorized, provided of course one knew one was in the presence of this natural camera that was presenting one with images. The photo, qua photo, stresses this. Even when it has nothing to do with death, the photograph indicates the absence of what is in the picture. It has the power, or perhaps in the West one should say, had the power, to evoke an irretrievable absence. In the early days of photography, people were often terrorized by the camera. Something of that attitude remains in *Pos Kota*.

But the photograph need not evoke absence as one knows from the way it is usually viewed today. *Pos Kota* tries to ensure that the photograph is the site or the sight of absence by its captions. It does so because its aim in *Pos Kota* is to establish a certain realm of terror or fascination, then to turn it into a story, and by doing so, to reestablish a social and political community by tracing the trajectory of "trauma," cure, and the need for political security.

As I have said, there are often as many as twenty photographs on the first page of *Pos Kota*. These photos are not the sort that we are accustomed to, first of all, because the camera itself often plays a role in the scenery. Take, for instance, the picture of Mrs. Herlin Widrastuti collapsed on a chair, surrounded by comforting women. The caption reads, "Mrs. Herlin Widrastuti sits drooping, embraced by a neighbor. For the moment, the baby is asleep." One wonders at the literalness of the caption that says so much one could understand merely by looking. But I believe the repetition of what one knows by seeing told in words is not accidental. It is a sign of the need felt to make sure the photograph does not speak for itself. The pictures are stiff and even stereotyped. They seem sometimes to be posed or arranged to show what one should see, as in the photograph of the coffin being carried to the grave. Rarely do they show spontaneous moments. There are no pictures of athletes caught in a moment only the camera could see. And *Pos Kota* does not hesitate to use the same picture a second time, as was the case with Serkap Bambang.

The pictures often identify. They seem to use photographs taken for that purpose as in the photograph of Serkap Bambang, which shows his head, face straight forward, with an expression appropriate for a police officer. Identification extends beyond the person to the scene. The caption under the first picture of Mrs. Widrastuti speaks of the baby who is "asleep for the moment." This is pure pathos. One does not need to wonder what happens in the next instant when the baby wakes up. The picture is complete in itself as it shows grief and communal consolation. Whatever one wonders about, it is not likely to be the various alternative actions that might have occurred after the picture was taken, at least so far as *Pos Kota* can help it; the artificial arrangement of persons, the pose, forbids that. The next moment, after the photograph is taken, is absorbed by the story. The baby is mentioned as part of a stereotyped story of grief, orphans, and widow. In a later story (2 September 1993) Mrs. Widrastuti speaks of how she must emerge from mourning to raise her children; another report of the same date tells how the older child comforts his mother. These pictures are arranged to fit notions not merely in the accompanying stories, but in themes frequently used previously in the paper.

Photographs such as the one we are speaking about show two figures who are, one says in English, "not in the picture." There is the baby who, when he awakes, will miss his father but who, for the moment, is unaware. There is Mrs. Widrastuti who is all too aware of her late husband and who, for that reason, cannot focus her mind on her surroundings. They both are meant to show that what one sees in the picture, the immediacy that is an attribute of photographs, is excluded from this picture. On the contrary, what is most important is what is outside the picture and, in any case, always invisible. The photograph shows this here by the references it makes to the frequent stories in *Pos Kota* that show the effects of "death."

But "death" here is not death as it was before this use of the photograph because the photograph relocates it. We repeat: death is not associated with ghosts in the ordinary sense in these cases. "Death" is placed "where one cannot see," or at least in some of the places "one cannot see." And it is the function of the photograph to establish that one cannot see. One cannot see something: the country of "death," danger, and criminals. It is a realm attached to *Pos Kota*'s stories of Jakarta and Indonesia.

These stereotyped arrangements are also susceptible to another sort of reading, one that escapes the notions of what one should see as repeated by the texts. In the picture I was describing, Mrs. Widrastuti is facing the camera, but she is not engaged by it or by anything visible. By contrast, the woman with her arms on her shoulders and the woman standing on the other side look at her full of concern. These, again, are stereotyped expressions, though not necessarily lacking force because of that. The women in the background look at the camera. That would not be odd if it were not for the question of where the camera is located. The presence of so many women in such close proximity to Mrs. Widrastuti makes one think that a space has been cleared for the photographer. The picture seems to be posed if we look at the women standing in the background. On the other hand, the picture of Mrs. Widrastuti herself does not have that appearance.

I believe that the scene was posed, but I think also that the camera here is part of the scene. It is unlike a snapshot where nothing is rearranged to accommodate the camera and where one feels that life is presented as it was come across and where the presence of the camera is forgotten. Here, there seems to have been a rearrangement, but nonetheless the qualities of the action—grief, reassurance, aide—are not made false. To see the suffering Mrs. Widrastuti is not an intrusion on an intense and private moment in her life. Grief is no longer an uncontrollable, spontaneous state that would be interrupted by asking the grieving person to move a little to the left. The camera has a place in the scene of mourning, even to the point of necessitating its rearrangement. The camera, though not visible, is made evident by the pose that, without the camera, would lack all coherence. Mourning is assimilated to a separate register appropriate to the camera.

On the opposite side of the page the camera is in front of pallbearers bearing the sergeant's coffin. The caption reads "The corpse of Serkap Bambang Sumarno being removed from Police Sector Pulogadung to be buried shortly after at the house of mourning of the R.I. Police Complex at K." For this picture, the photographer stood in the path of the procession. It is again a formal shot—the coffin on the shoulders of the pallbearers in formal police dress while in the background there are ranks of saluting, uniformed police. But the space occupied by the camera plays a part in the picture, just as it does with the photo of the grieving widow. It is on the path leading out of the complex, in the space between the cortege and the gate. Here the photographer has not rearranged anything. If one reads the caption, the body is being carried to the police complex. But if one looks at the photograph, it is being carried into the camera, delivered into the photograph.

One might think that this is merely a technical question and that nothing should be made of it. But *Pos Kota* photographs have a certain independence from the texts that accompany them. For instance, there is often symmetry or opposition between photographs. In the issue of the paper last cited, on one side of the page there is the widow, mourning and comforted by police wives, and on the other, the corpse of her husband in his coffin saluted by his colleagues, who are presumably the husbands of those wives seen on the other side of the page. Wives and husbands are arranged alike in ranks in the background of both pictures. In another issue (4 September 1993) there is a photo on the left-hand side of the page showing one of the criminals being interrogated while on the other side a photo shows the ill villager who put out the fire burning the body showing deep respect to a police officer. Here the opposition is police as interrogators of criminals versus police as rewarders of those with civic virtue. The photograph of Mrs. Widrastuti being comforted is partially reproduced in another issue. The others have been cropped out and she appears, on the other side of the page from the original use of the picture, isolated in her grief, and facing right instead of left. The most telling example occurs in an issue that shows two suspects on the left while on the right in another picture a police chief makes a speech. The picture shows him with his hand raised, finger extended, in a gesture of warning that can easily be taken to be addressed to the criminals across the page. The photographs thus have a certain independence of the text, even to the point of sometimes seeming to communicate with each other. It is as though the characters pictured live a life in photographs different from the one their originals lived in actual life.

Again, it is similar to the world of ghosts. I can explain this by telling of my own ghostly encounter with *Pos Kota*. Photocopying from microfilm, one copy came out white on black instead of black on white. The librarian could not explain why. He could only suppose that it was caused by *Pos Kota*. The machine is supposed to sense which is dark and which light and print accordingly, automatically, but, he said, the large number of photographs fooled the machine and it printed in reverse. The *Pos Kota* camera senses what is background and what is substance, sometimes reversing the order to create a world where everyone photographed, not merely criminals, comes to lead a second, ghostly life. But their second existence is in a world of technology distinguished from the world of ordinary ghosts.

This, no doubt, is exaggeration, but I am trying to construct the possible readings of *Pos Kota* and to account for the prominent place of photographs in the paper. In this story and many others, they are strongly associated with "death," the dead, the place of "death," the possibility not of seeing what they picture but of indicating that one cannot see, or one can see only to a certain point. The large number of pictures on the front page means that the pictures are necessarily small, so small and, no doubt for technical reasons, so indistinct that it is difficult to make out exactly what is pictured. But if there is any question about whether one can see what might be there or not, it is resolved by pictures of criminals. For decades *Pos Kota* showed all those arrested with a black band across their eyes. Then they stopped doing so. According to the managing editor, they put the band there not for legal reasons, but because otherwise it might cause embarrassment. The person might not be guilty or even if he were, his family would be embarrassed. Soon people understood that those pictured were in fact guilty. So they showed suspects without the supplied mask in order to indicate that simply by looking at the pictures one could not be sure whether it was a criminal one was seeing or not. They wanted to indicate that seeing photographs and understanding them are different. Given that in the rhetoric of *Pos Kota* every person reported arrested is assumed to be a criminal where that word means an exemplification of kriminalitas, guilt and innocence here have a quasireligious sense, indicating techno-spectral-photographic origins rather than legal status.

The logic of *Pos Kota* photographs repeats that of witnesses. Mrs. Widrastuti wanted to see the faces of her husband's murderers. She did not want to understand, only to see without penetration, to see only to the point where, beyond that, one cannot see further. *Pos Kota,* in other words, uses photographs not to actually obscure, but to indicate a limit to vision. In doing so, they imply something beyond that limit that, again, is not precisely the realm of ghosts but is its analogue in being elsewhere, removed from life, and associated with "death." But the photograph not only conceals, it also reveals; or it does both at the same time, so that occasionally what is concealed appears to live a second time in the picture. It is like a ghost, but a new sort of ghost, a ghost of technology.

Thus there is tension between photographs and captions. To the degree that the caption exhausts or seems to exhaust what the photograph shows, whatever might be imagined to be beyond the limit established by the picture is accounted for. One sees the police looking at the bare patch of ground, seeing nothing at all and one knows because one is told so that they are thinking hard and about to take charge of the case. There is, as the police doctor told the villager suffering from "trauma," nothing to worry about. "Don't think too much about what happened, *pak*. Its all in the hands of the police now." ("tidak usah terlalu pikirkan kejadian itu, Pak, semuanya sudah ditangani polisi." 4 September 1983). It is possible to look at the photographs and to be fascinated by them, to be absorbed to a point where reading the story does not stop one from continuing to look at the pictures. It is, no doubt, why the editors who began with short accounts decided to have longer stories. Otherwise readers could not dismiss what they read in the way that all newspaper readers must in order to get on with the day. One sees men sitting on the curb with *Pos Kota*, spending time with their papers, removed from the world in a way that one misses in readers of the New York papers on the subway. Readers in New York subways are alert to their neighbors even if their reading is a way to avoid having to acknowledge their awareness. Middle class Indonesians are embarrassed to think that they might be thought to be as absorbed as their lower class compatriots; they claim not to read *Pos Kota*.

The camera in *Pos Kota* is sometimes a magical instrument. One sees this in the picture of the funeral cortege marching not into the camera but into the picture, as though the time of the photo was dual. On the one hand, the photographer was there when the picture was taken and what we see occurred earlier. But on the other hand, the cortege is present in the photo at the moment one sees it. To read the picture the first way is to be convinced by the caption and the text. To read it the second way is to think that the photograph is appropriate to "death," that the corpse is carried from police headquarters through the camera into the picture. It appears in a now, a present that is an effect of photography. This reading can well be congruent with the first. It says in effect that the realm of "death" is connected with those who control technology; thus, we might be grateful to the police who protect us from technological phantoms or negatives, as it were.

The police doctor tells the man suffering from "trauma" not to think too much about the event. It is what Mrs. Widrastuti also wants when she asks to see the face of IA. If she can see without understanding, she has stopped thinking. She knows she cannot understand more and yet she has preserved something of her husband. As the agent of the sergeant's death IA was the last to see the sergeant alive. Seeing IA's face, Mrs. Widrastuti gains something back of her husband and at the same time ceases to think about him. IA here is the camera that in *Pos Kota* allows people to see that they cannot see and to know that they cannot understand further. This makes the murderer himself an embodiment of the camera. He fixes something of the person he killed, captures something of him, and transfers it to the widow. Mourning, a process in which involuntary memories arise in order to be put back into the past where they will no longer disturb, is short-circuited by the witness and the *Pos Kota* photograph.

But there is no necessity in the construction of the camera, by virtue of its technology, for it to be the instrument that shows that one cannot see further. Were that the case, interpretations of photography would be the same everywhere. There are only possibilities inherent in it. The camera makes something appear and causes the viewer to think about invisibility. But it could also be that one would think only that it shows what was there accurately, without distortion, that it is an instrument of representation, and that this representation is a purely technical matter. Or one could think that the absence indicated by the photograph has nothing to do with "death," but is the place of any number of imaginative constructions or of none at all. One's reading of photographs is learned; the photograph as such is indecipherable. It allows various interpretations to be put on the status of what it does not show, only one of which is that there is a boundary between visible and invisible and that there is existence on each side.

The line of interpretation that keeps open all possibilities is for that very reason controllable by no one. The readers of *Pos Kota* who are fascinated by imagery, who cannot put it into words, find themselves in an imaginative register that is not subject to the power of the editors or the police. This does not make them exemplars of resistance. They resist nothing; they are merely somewhere else for a while; a somewhere else that cannot be equated even with "death." They may be the best readers, or they may remain merely fascinated, that is, stupefied, but they are also politically disabled. In any case, they are the ones who make it necessary for the editors to have long stories to ensure that the fascination of the photograph is replaced by the social reality conveyed by the text.

Thus there are multiple ways to read these photographs. One has to keep in mind *Pos Kota*'s readers. They are often people recently arrived in the city from the countryside, so they are often first-generation newspaper readers. That is, they are readers for whom the conventions of newspaper reading are not firmly established. It is for that reason also that they need long stories. Without them, the photographs can mean too much. If one does not assume this, one has difficulty in understanding how, in a place where there is no culture of the book, where reading is not particularly valued, a country without a significant literary scene, where newspapers are devoid of news, nonetheless people want long stories. The question is how ways of reading become limited. The answer I am suggesting is through the figure of the new criminal.

Let us return to the motive in the case under consideration.[1] IA wanted the instrument of power. Not merely the pistol but what in *Pos Kota* is called the vital instrument, the alat vital, the penis. Alat is the Indonesian word for tool or instrument in the generic sense. In other words, he wanted the tool that creates life, that makes things appear. *Pos Kota*, following the general linguistic usage of the press, makes the penis equivalent to the pistol, a piece of technology, a tool. But it is a special one because vital instrument, in Indonesian as in English, is not only a necessary tool, but also an instrument that makes life. With the two tools, the pistol and the vital instrument, IA symbolically has the power to make appear and to make disappear. He is a murderer, but, appearing to villagers who saw him in another technological guise, the new red car, he caused them to appear in the photos of *Pos Kota* and thus, one can say, in the eyes of the nation. It is from this perspective that I want to suggest again that IA embodies the power of the camera.[2]

IA is the figure control of whom means control of the multiple possibilities of representation. But he is never entirely mastered. He makes neglected villagers recognizable by the Indonesian world, visiting them as he did and being responsible for their appearance in the newspapers. The police come on to the scene later. They do not control him, as he will appear with other initials to other villagers again. But they assuage his effects. In his multiple forms he remains at large making the police necessary, just as he himself steals a portion of his instruments from them. The upper-class criminal is not always distinguishable from the officers of the state, such as the president, who claim to control him.

This new criminal type inheres in the nation, fascinating it. It is out of fascination with his power, one surmises, that Mrs. Widrastuti wants to see her husband's assassin. What she has lost and what her husband lost, a certain power, is found again in his murderer. She presumably saw him in life. The readers of the paper never saw him, his photograph never appeared, perhaps because of the intervention of his stepfather. But they see their president's picture, reproduced each day in the paper, and can reproduce Mrs. Widrastuti's experience. The photograph magnifies the power of the murderer and thus seems to borrow its power from him. But the converse is also true. The power of the camera to make someone or something appear and disappear is set within the story of criminals and thus becomes subject to control.

IA seems to differ from President Suharto. The former drew his force from the police, the latter, as we understand him, from the criminals of kriminalitas. But one has to see the two as parts of a single ideal type. IA shows that power, meaning symbolic power, rests with the upper class, even outside constituted Indonesian political structures. Precisely as such this class has not only the apparatus of force but also the ability to haunt those who once made up "the people." Through the adoption of terms such as "trauma" and "shock," this modern haunting shows that, really, the underclass belongs to the same symbolic world as its rulers. It is precisely out of fear that it does not, that it remains outside their ken, that the underclass is in turn positioned to haunt its rulers. Power that remains outside established circuits passes and repasses between classes, putting itself fatally in evidence.

Kriminalitas has several sources. The criminal as a locus of power was generated through ideas of illegitimacy and through the history of "the people" before and after the revolution. But kriminalitas is an effect of the press and in particular of its cameras and it would not exist without it, in my opinion. This does not mean that there would be no massacres and no counter revolution without kriminalitas. There would still be a specter haunting Indonesia, the effect of the absence of "the people." This specter is brought into view by the power of technological revelation and given a form by kriminalitas. The camera brings into view images that, precisely in their capacity to conceal and reveal at the same time, after the fact show that there is something inherent in the nation. Something seems to lurk within Indonesia and it becomes the object of those avid for its power, generating the new criminal type.

The camera has to be understood first as a rhetorical device showing the locus of a new idea, "death." It begins as an apparatus of supplementarity, showing after the fact that there is something inherent in the tattooed body, in the criminal. It surpasses the conventional limits of rhetoric, however, because it delivers an image that is open to such a large range of interpretation. New stories emerge through photographs, not to mention the accounts that take new paths once a corpse is found. One sees how by considering words such as "trauma," "shock," sadis, and serious. These are words the readers of *Pos Kota* are not likely to have known initially, not knowing English. They arrive to readers as configurations of ink, not so different from the configurations incised on the skins of Petrus victims. Their murderers discarded the intended sense of their victims' tattoos, seeing them merely as indications of force. Like Petrus victims' tattoos, these untranslated words have force. They show villagers, rather than say to them, that their suffering is ununderstandable. They mean, each time, "I do not know what is causing my sickness," or "I do not know what is likely to return to hurt or kill me." But these words are not translated and therefore it is not their sense that matters. It is, rather, that in the narratives of death as it occurs between classes, there is a point of incomprehension around which phantasms are generated. Such words are given a place in the vocabulary of Indonesian without being truly assimilated to the language. The camera locates this power in the national landscape. (*Pos Kota* has almost no pictures from abroad.) No matter what interpretations one makes of photographs, they all have their locus in the nation. If the force inherent in the communication of such words were not, with the aide of the camera, claimed to be found within the nation, the continuing menace of revolution as the upper classes feel it might be less violently assuaged.

There is thus an additional process other than the one we have described in this book. In addition to the relations of family and nation and the historical questions of nationalism and revolution, there is also untranslated mediation. Asharudin's nephew when he became unrecognizable embodied the force of kriminalitas, yet another foreign word within Indonesian. Such moments, amplified in Petrus and said to erupt into daily life, bring about proxysisms of national selfconsciousness and their remedies.[3]

It is here also that we can locate "trauma," a word foreign to the Indonesian language, in Indonesia. Certain villagers had pains. They felt these pains had a connection with the burned corpse of the policeman but they knew they did not know how this could be. They (or the newspaper) therefore resorted to the word trauma, already arrived from abroad. "Trauma" indicates a physical condition, a mark on the body, whose cause is unlocatable but is nevertheless, by the foreignness of the word, associated with things foreign. Those so marked are susceptible to being retrieved into the nation via the work of authorities who claim to understand this word.

When one looks at a photograph, one assumes that the horizon of one's everyday world is displaced; one sees something from another time and probably another place. This shift of horizon is also the condition for the use of the word trauma in Indonesia. Indonesian "trauma" is appropriable, curable even, and thus not trauma in the strict psychoanalytic usage. If there was no cure for "trauma" in Indonesia, much that is culturally and politically essential would be different. But "trauma" is claimed to be curable in Indonesia, and is thus available for political control. This availability rests on its conveyances, the corpse, and the camera. The corpse as a conveyer of effects originating beyond one's horizon is knowable as such to the readers of *Pos Kota* via the camera. In the process of being announced, the place of death is reestablished. It is no longer marked by ghosts but by the limit of photographic visibility. Once delimited, the police take charge.

Some words from the time of the revolution, notably revolution (revolusi), were derived from foreign origins. But these words became central to the formation of the Indonesian language. As Anderson pointed out, they took the place of Dutch equivalents that, when used by Indonesians, frequently left the users divorced from their fellow countrymen who could not speak Dutch. When converted into Indonesian, which means being given an Indonesian ending rather than being translated, the word allowed leaders and followers to be conjoined. Revolusi, along with certain other words, not necessarily of foreign origin, contained the aspirations of the nation, even if these were not spelled out. By contrast, "shock," "trauma," and other foreign words now current indicate only fear and point merely to pain. This pain is the indicator that the words do not belong to the language. They mark the place where something of foreign origin has arrived in Indonesia but is mere interruption, unconnected not merely to aspirations but to the daily activities of those whom the words mark.[4] However that may be, the labeling of the event left it open for the police to solve not the crime but the "trauma," thus reestablishing these villagers in the nation.

"Trauma," "shock," kriminalitas indicate a foreign origin for something found domestically and the possibility also of control of that foreignness by the present political class. But the foreignness indicated is misleading. It is generated inside Indonesia by the failure of its revolution and by the camera. When, emerging from the family, men (women are seldom invoked) cannot find a place in the nation, in a certain fashion they are made foreign to it. "Revolusi" made villagers part of the Indonesian nation. The revolutionary impulse in Indonesia has not abated. But its force now marks its bearers as different kinds of beings. National forces stemming from above cause villagers senseless pain or "trauma"; kriminalitas, also a national force, arises from within villagers and other members of the lower class. It delivers the latter into national society and makes them seemingly identical to their neighbors and relatives. It leaves them Indonesians of a special sort. It is implicit in the journals that the criminals of kriminalitas are uncanny, like "us" but spectral. It was in their uncanny national identity, rather than as foreigners, as Croats became to Serbs and Hutus to Tutsis, that they were murdered.

Criminals and revolutionaries in present day Indonesian rhetoric share a spectral quality indicating that death is their place of origin. The Indonesian counter-revolution is not a case of one class taking back what another gained. To find the criminals of kriminalitas is to prevent revolution not merely by acting against figures who, transformed, emerge from the past, but by addressing a source supposed common to both revolutionaries and the criminals of kriminalitas. Their commonality is not only a matter of class. They are effects of untranslated words that change with the changes of regime. Their reception most recently has been shaped by the work of the camera. The camera is the chief instrument of definition of this "death," which is their provenance.

The camera of *Pos Kota* is an instrument of counter-revolution. But for the criminals of kriminalitas to be suppressed they must also appear. The types who appear in faits divers could once again become politically significant, even revolutionary. The camera can be thought, in capturing the criminal and the corpse, the revolutionary and the "traumatized" to be registering the essence of things, as Benjamin put it. No one can read that essence, he comments. But those pictured bear its mark.

Notes

Introduction

1 For reports on these killings see John Pemberton, *On the Subject of "Java"* (Ithaca: Cornell University Press, 1994), pp. 311–318; and Justus van der Kroef, " 'Petrus': Patterns of Prophylactic Murder in Java," *Asian Survey* 25, no. 7 (July 1985): 745–759. Van der Kroef quotes the director of the Indonesian Legal Aid Society as estimating the numbers killed at 8500. This report was issued some months before the killings came to an end.

2 For an interpretation of the role of translation and stories of criminals in Indonesian nationalism, see Pramoedya Ananta Toer, *Tempo Doeloe*, (Jakarta: Hasta Mitra, 1982) as well as Siegel, *Fetish, Recognition, Revolution* (Princeton: Princeton University Press, 1997). Pramoedya Ananta Toer has an important discussion of the role of the lingua franca in the development of Indonesian nationalism. It is contained in various articles in the newspaper for which he wrote before it was closed down by the government. A list of these articles can be found in footnote 3 to the Introduction of Siegel, *Fetish, Recognition, Revolution*. For the history of criminals in one section of Indonesia during the revolution see Robert Cribb, *Gangsters and Revolutionaries: The Jakarta People's Militia and the Indonesian Revolution of 1945–1949* (Sydney: Allen & Unwin, 1991).

3 The history of the Indonesian revolution has two strands. One led to independence from Dutch rule via negotiation. The other, led by youths, was without national organization or much ideological coherence and was more radical in its demands and more violent in its actions. B.R.O.'G. Anderson recounts the second of these in *Java in a Time of Revolution*, (Ithaca: Cornell University Press, 1972). It is the story of how youths forced their national leaders into more extreme stances, including the proclamation of independence. Youthful revolutionaries threatened also to displace the Indonesian political class left in place after the Japanese occupation, itself the heir of colonial policies. Anderson's study of the role of youth in the revolution, showing as it does their independence from recognized national leaders and their revolutionary tendencies, is part of the foundation of the present work. The early study by George Kahin, *Nationalism and Revolution in Indonesia* (Ithaca: Cornell University Press, 1952) detailed the rise of nationalism and the history of the revolutionary period focusing on its leaders.

The immense question of popular participation in nationalism and revolution has been treated from different points of view. Recent regional studies include most notable Audrey Kahin (ed.), *Regional Dynamics of the Indonesian Revolution: Unity from Diver-*

sity, (Ithaca: Cornell University Press, 1985). A synopsis of accepted views of the course of the revolution after Kahin with bibliographic references can be found in Anthony J. S. Reid, *The Indonesian National Revolution* (Hawthorn, Victoria: Longman Australia, 1974). Quite important because it points the way to understanding the formation of nationalist ideas as they mediated regional origins is the study of Rudolf Mrazek, *Sjahrir, Prolitics and Exile in Indonesia* (Ithaca: Cornell Southeast Asia Program, 1994). Mrazak's pioneering work opens the way to a wholly new sort of study of the formation of the nation.

4 There were, for example, reports of blank sheets of paper found in communist headquarters that, it was claimed, were lists of those targeted for death by the communists, readable if one had the right chemical formula to develop the writing. Stories of such lists were widespread at the time, but there is no reliable evidence of their existence. See Anderson and McVey, *A Preliminary Analysis of the 1965 Coup in Indonesia* (Ithaca: Cornell Modern Indonesia Project, 1971), n. 2, part 2, p. 116.

5 The term "organizations without form" (*organisasi tanpa bentuk'*) has some interesting usages. In 1988 Attorney General Ali Said banned a book by Pramoedya Ananta Toer, Indonesia's most accomplished writer, the latter a political prisoner for fourteen years and, like 80,000 others suspected of being communists, never brought to trial. The attorney general stated that the book was an example of the "infiltration of society which went unfelt by it." He went to say that the communists had now decided that "organizations without form are best." (Kompas, Ali Said, 10 June 1988). The head of an Indonesian intelligence agency, General Sudomo, said Pramoedya's book was "a form of instruction and reference book for PKI [Indonesian Communist Party] members and their sympathizers." For him, Pramoedya's book was code book. Break the code and one sees, behind, within the lines, its true sense. "The conclusion that this book contains Marxism and Marxism-Leninism was reached after careful and deep consideration." He added that if these teachings "are not wiped out, it is obvious that public order will be at an end." (Jayakarta, Sudomo, 10 June 1988)

In 1995, thirty years after the killings of accused communists, Lt. General Soeyono, speaking for the Coordinating Body for National Stability (known by its acronym Bakorstanas), said

> problems raised by the PKI (Indonesian Communist Party) now are being brought to the surface again by certain groups who agitate as they did. We have to anticipate.

What he anticipated was of course what he claimed had occurred already and which he said could easily occur again. He "anticipated," without giving evidence, that the people involved would be or are the grandchildren of the dead communists. A reporter from the magazine *Tiras* asked him if there were indications (*indikasi*) of PKI agitation.

> The clearest indicator (*indikator*) is that the struggle is the same and there is a red line from the family too. Maybe from grandchildren who hope to revenge their ancestors. This is what we detect now. (Interview entitled "Skenario dan Agitasi yang Sama," [The Same Scenario and Agitation], *Tiras* 37, no. 1 [12 October 1995]: 63. I am indebted to Takashi Shiraishi for calling my attention to this article.)

Asked for the symptoms, the general added that this form of detection (*terdeteksi*) was general. The year of the interview, 1995, was also the year in which General Soeyono, repeating the 1988 claim of the attorney general, again accused Pramoedya Ananta Toer and others of inspiring organizations without form (*organisasi tanpa bentuk'*), which carried out activities resembling those of communists. (François Raillon, "Indonésie

1995: La République quinquagénaire," *Archipel* 51 [1996]: 179–196.) As the reporters of the newsmagazine *Tiras* put it, paraphrasing the words of another general, General R. Hartono, "There's no getting around it, we have to really set up our radar and be on the alert." "The New Left: Is it the Vehicle for a Comeback?" *Tiras* 37, no. 1 (12 October 1995): 64. To be on the alert for what has already happened is, of course, another version of the fear of vengeance, as the generals stated. But revenge that comes through spectral organizations and code books such as Pramoedya's work, is a strange sort.

6   One always has to except Pramoedya Ananta Toer from this statement. He continued to publish abroad when his books were banned in Indonesia. For remarks on the attitude of former prisoners, see my obituary of Joebar Ayoeb, *Indonesia* 62 (October 1996).

7   On the subject of the rallies and the early development of nationalism, see the important book of Takashi Shiraishi, *An Age in Motion* (Ithaca: Cornell University Press, 1990).

8   Here it is of some value to consult the dictionaries. No major dictionary of Indonesian has an entry for kriminalitas before 1983, perhaps because early dictionaries of Indonesian often did not include words derived from European languages. I thank Daniel Lev for telling me that the word occurred in the Sukarno period, though its use clearly was much restricted by comparison with the Suharto period. In 1983, during the New Order, the *Kamus Bahasa Indonesia* [Dictionary of Indonesian] (Jakarta: Pusat Pembinaan dan Pembangunan Bahasa Deptemen Pendidikan dan Kebudayaan, 1983) gave this definition:

kriminalitas *n:* events with a criminal character; acts which violate the criminal law; bad deeds; in this archipelago, robbery, armed smuggling and sales of various drugs are reflected in statistics.

The same dictionary has the entry kriminal with the definition "bad deeds (violation of the law) which can be judged according to statutes." By contrast, the major Indonesian dictionary of the Sukarno period, which, as I have said, has no entry for kriminalitas, gives this for kriminil: "bad deeds (violations of the law which can be judged according to statutes)." W.J.S. Poerwadarminta, *Kamus Umum Bahasa Indonesia*, 4th edition (Jakarta: Balai Pustaka, 1966).

It is worth noting that the term I have translated as bad deeds, *kejahatam* is a word in everyday use that reflects standards of behavior derived from common sense, the heir of traditional and religious ideas. One translation includes sinful for instance. If one looks at the substance of kriminalitas judged by its appearance in newspapers, it consists mainly of robbery, rape, incest, fraud, and murder. If the substance of the idea is known and if it already has a name—kejahatam—one has to ask why it was given another name. Furthermore, one has to ask why this new name is not Indonesian. A new signifier, known to be foreign, comes to denote an indigenous idea. The implication is that there is a further reference, one beyond whatever one might delimit by making an inventory of particular acts that fall under kejahatam.

Previous to the New Order, bad deeds were not criminal unless the law was invoked. The blurring of the boundary between bad deeds and criminal acts reflects the resurgence not of earlier concepts but of sentiments attributable to prenational times, which are, one can say, nationalized. The question is what nationalization means in this context.

9   For an excellent discussion of faits divers, see Roland Barthes, "Qu'est-ce qu'un scandale?" in Roland Barthes, *Oeuvres complètes*, Éric Marty, ed. (Paris: éditions du Seuil, 1995), vol. 1, pp. 784–786; (originally published in *Lettres Nouvelles*, 4 March 1959); and "Structure du fait divers," in Barthes, *Oeuvres Completes*, pp. 1309–1316; (originally published in *Médiations*, 1962).

1   Illegitimacy and "the People"

1   Sukarno, *An Autobiography: As Told to Cindy Adams* (Jakarta: Gunung Agung, 1965), pp. 18–20.

2   *Soeharto, Pikiran, Ucapkan, dan Tindakan Saya: Otobiografi seperti dipaparkan kepada G. Dwipayana dan Ramadhan K. H.* [*My Thoughts, Speech, and Acts: Autobiography as told to G. Dwipayana and Ramadhan K. H.*], ed. G. Dwipayana and Ramadhan K. H. (Jakarta: PT Citra Lamtoro Gung Persada, 1988).

3   For a discussion of racial and legal classifications in the Dutch East Indies, see C. Fasseur, "Cornerstone and Stumbling Block: Racial Classification and the Late Colonial State in Indonesia" in Robert Cribb (ed.), *The Late Colonial State in Indonesia: Political and Economic Foundations of the Netherlands Indies 1880–1942*, (Leiden: KITLV Press, 1994), pp. 31–56.

4   The quotation is taken from a longer citation in the excellent account of Daniel S. Lev, *Islamic Courts in Indonesia: A Study in the Political Basis of Legal Institutions*, (Berkeley: University of California Press, 1972), p. 23.

5   Compare B.R.O'G. Anderson, writing on Indonesian, saying that it "represented in essence a 'project,' an aspiration to unity and equality, a generous wager on the future— in the face of some increasingly intractable social facts." "The Languages of the Indonesian Politics," *Indonesia* 1 (1966). Anderson explains how Indonesian, arising as a new language, taking the place of Dutch as the vehicle of nationalist thinking and becoming the national language, lacked the resonances of Javanese that had grown over time and in seclusion. Indonesian, by contrast, was a language of the present and the future. It made possible a link between the modernity of the West and the universe of the Indies that Dutch did not. Indonesians who learned Dutch found themselves in a Dutch universe, unable to communicate with fellow Indonesians who did not know the language. Indonesian bridged the gap between worlds in part by generating heavily charged words that promised access to that world for Indonesians, but left the content obscure. On the role of parents in this transition, see Siegel, *Fetish, Recognition, Revolution*.

6   For a discussion of this as seen in nationalist novels, see Siegel *Fetish, Recognition, Revolution*, (Princeton: Princeton University Press, 1997), chaps. 4–6.

7   Sometimes it is the mother who is at fault, for instance, for insisting on parental prerogatives in the choice of marriage partners for her children. In this case it is not the weakness of parents, but their misguided strength. The disastrous effects show the inability of nationalist children simply to turn their backs on the parents, just as Sukarno, we will see, insisted on the permanent debt he owed his mother.

8   John Legge, *Sukarno: A Political Biography* (London: Allen Lane, Penguin Press, 1972), p. 19.

9   The performative is described by J. L. Austin, *How to do Things with Words*, (Cambridge: Harvard University Press, 1962).

10 On the use of familial terms outside the family see Kenji Tsuchiya, *Democracy and Leadership: The Rise of the Taman Siswa Movement in Indonesia* (Peter Hawkes, trans.) (Honolulu: University of Hawaii Press, 1987), and Saya Shiraishi, *The Young Heros: The Indonesian Family and Politics* (Ithaca: Cornell Southeast Asia Program, 1997). In seminars we gave together, Takashi Shiraishi pointed out the lineage-like quality of Indonesian political and social networks.

11 On this question see *The Seminar of Jacques Lacan: Book Three, The Psychosis, 1955–56*,

Jacques-Alain Miller (ed.), Russell Grigg (trans.) (New York: Norton, 1993). Here I want also to acknowledge the influence of Book 7 of Lacan's seminar: *The Ethics of Psychoanalysis, 1959–1960,* Jacques-Alain Miller (ed.), Dennis Porter (trans.) (London: Routledge, 1992) in conceiving the law in retrospect. Lacan, of course, reinflected the works of Freud.

John Pemberton pointed out to me that the word rakyat has scarcely disappeared today but when it is used it is only to refer to an absent body. The performative, making the rakyat appear, has disappeared and with it also the figure of the rakyat as, for instance, an actor in social events, even when it is used to speak of something off stage. The criminal of kriminalitas does not fully replace the rakyat, making only an incipient appearance.

2 Bastards, Revolution, and Kriminalitas

1 The paper was the subject of telling comments by B.R.O'G. Anderson, "Cartoons and Monuments" in Anderson, *Language and Politics* (Ithaca: Cornell University Press, 1994)
2 Interview with Ny. Sugiarto, 7 December 1987.
3 "Polisi Tembak Mati Atasan" *Pos Kota,* 25 May 1983.
4 The *Pos Kota* version is by S. Saiful Rahim. S. Saiful Rahim, *Perjalanan Hidup Kusni Kasdut,* (Jakarta: Pustaka Antar Kota, 1980), hereafter cited as SSR. The other is a fictionalized version: Parakitri, *Kusni Kasdut* (Jakarta: Gramedia, 1979), hereafter cited as Par. The fictionalization, according to a note of the author, "is based on the true story of Kusni Kasdut" (no page number) and seems to consist mainly in the addition of dialogue. S. Saiful Rahim has supplied no dialogue, but he does not hesitate to give Kusni's reactions to events as they were at the time. I have followed both accounts, which seem to be based equally on interviews with Kusni and do not differ greatly in their lines of interpretation though some events are included in only one or the other of these books. Whether these interpretations are due to Kusni or to the authors, I cannot say for certain. In any case, what concerns us is the construction of a story for the press, rather than the reality of Kusni's life.
5 Parakitri says this outright (p. 58). S. Saiful Rahim pictures Kusni as disappointed when he learns what his mother tells him of his father is not true and shows him trying to find out the facts. In the latter account, Kusni is first bitter toward his mother for lying to him and then, when he finds out that she did so in order to give him pride in his descent, he determines to raise the respect shown him. SSR (15–29; the chapter entitled "Inner Conflict")
6 S. Saiful Rahim leaves out the account that follows of Kusni Kasdut's involvement with communist women and thus lacks the important dimension of his relation to the Indonesian Communist Party. In its place he emphasizes Kusni's relation to his wife.
7 This is likely to be a pseudonym, Parakitri mentioning that names have been changed in accordance with Kusni Kasdut's wishes.
8 For stories from the time of the massacres see Anderson and McVey, *A Preliminary Analysis of the October 1965 Coup in Indonesia* (Ithaca: Cornell Modern Indonesia Project, 1971). For stories from the time of the revolution see Matu Mona, *Peristiwa demi Peristiwa* (Medan: Pustaka Anugrah, n.d.; probably written in the 1950s).
9 Kusni's other famous crime was the abduction of a wealthy man from whom he asked ransom. During his trial he claimed that the man was giving money to the Darul Islam,

the insurgent Islamic group of the time. The defense failed and Kusni was sentenced to death, eventually to have his sentence commuted. It is worth noting that this crime was committed during the Sukarno period. Compare *Tempo* "Is it True that He was a member of Satan's Army?" (29 September 1979): 53–55. In this report doubt is cast on Kusni's revolutionary activities.

10   For a picture of Kusni as husband and father, see "Kusni, the Husband, the Father," in *Tempo*, 29 September 1979. On the jago see Onghokham, *The Residency of Madiun: Priyayi and Peasant in 19th Century Java*, (Ph.D. dissertation, Yale University, New Haven, 1975); Henk Schulte Nordholt, "The Jago in the Shadow: Crime and 'Order' in the Colonial State in Java," *Review of Indonesian and Malaysian Affairs*, 25 (1991), with its bibliography as well as his paper submitted to the conference on criminality in Southeast Asia held in Amsterdam in March 1997, written with Margreet van Till, "Colonial Criminals on Java 1870–1910." On the Philippines see John Sidel, "The Philippines: The Languages of Legitimation" in Muthiah Alagappa (ed.), *Political Legitimacy in Southeast Asia: The Quest for Moral Authority* (Stanford: Stanford University Press, 1995) and "The Usual Suspects: Nardong Putik, Don Pepe Oyson, and Robin Hood," paper submitted to the conference on criminality in Southeast Asia held in Amsterdam, March 1997. On the role of bandits and other such types in the Indonesian revolution see Robert Cribb, *Gangsters and Revolutionaries: The Jakarta People's Militia and the Indonesian Revolution of 1945–1949* (Sydney: Allen and Unwin, 1991).

11   At this point I want to bring to the reader's attention a remarkable short story written by Pramoedya Ananta Toer during the revolution entitled "Illegitimate Child" ("Anak Haram") in *Tjerita Dari Blora* (Djakarta: P.N. Balai Pustaka, 1963). In this story Pramoedya foresees a time after the revolution when the child of the Dutch collaborator is accused of illegitimacy. In this story the revolution, rather than marriage, governs the question of legitimacy of descent and leads to crime. It is, in part, through the influence of this story that I began to think of the issues I have discussed here.

3   In Lieu of "the People"

1   This report, unlike the others cited from *Tempo*, is under the heading "Law."

2   The classical description of the Javanese spirit world is Clifford Geertz, *The Religion of Java*, (Glencoe: The Free Press, 1960).

3   Sadis appears for the first time in a major Indonesian dictionary in the *Kamus Bahasa Indonesia*, (Jakarta: Departemen Pendidikan dan Kebudayan, 1983).

4   For another piece on the monstrosity of children as a reflection of the monstrous power of the attraction of money, see the *Tempo* article of 16 April 1983: 56; In this piece children, like Muralam, do not have the proper recognition of power. The difference is the distribution of forces. Money attracts them too greatly and the police create no fear in them.

5   Di Atas Garis Kenakalan Remaja, *Tempo*, 7 May 1983.

6   See, for instance, the important article of Ben Amar Mediane, "Alloula et les enfants: L'algerie du FLN au FIS," *Les Temps Modernes* 580 (Jan.–Feb., 1995): 10–23.

7   At this point I want to make a remark about the relation of kriminalitas to the expansion of the market in Indonesia. Indonesia in the New Order has seen a remarkable growth of the market economy. One would think that this might produce two reactions. One would be a resistance to foreign influence of the sort Sukarno expressed. Another would be a retreat to "authentic" identities in face of the possibility of finding

oneself an effect of the market. The latter has happened, but it has not been the case in general; nor has there been opposition of any significance to the intrusion of the market. Of course, one has to take account of the strict political control that dampens such reactions. But the lack of overt opposition to the market is also, in my opinion, because commodity fetishism is replaced, or perhaps disguised, by kriminalitas. One set of fears replaces another.

4   A New Criminal Type in Jakarta

1   One should note that castration has been a favorite topic of the press and movies for several years now.

2   I call them that because in *Pos Kota,* there are stories almost exclusively of arrests. One seldom gets to the trials. It is assumed that the police arrest the correct person. An editor of *Pos Kota* told me that the trial takes place such a long time after the arrest that people have lost interest. Justice is left out of the story.

3   On the way Jakartan rumors spread, see my "I Was Not There, But. . . .", *Archipel* 46 (1993).

4   "Utom (48) anggota Kamra Kampung Pasir Angin satu-satunya warga yang memamdamkan apai pembakar jenazah Serka Bambang Sumarno, kini dalam keadaan sakit keras. Dia mengaku karena trauma oleh peristiwa yang sangat meggemparkan itu."

5   For an account of this case written for the middle class, see the very abbreviated report in *Tempo,* "Intentions are one thing, realizations another" (11 September 1993). Here the murder was an accident, the youths merely seeking to prove their daring and to get some money by "borrowing" the sergeant's pistol. There is no mention of ghosts, trauma, castration, witnesses, or any of the other topics important to our analysis. It is an example of *Tempo*'s frequent attempt to make "them" just like "us," the readers. In the end, it is no less sinister than the stories of *Pos Kota,* murder happening by chance and the boys being similar to the readers' children. *Tempo* also gives the name of IA (Iman Al Amin) and his picture, without a bar across his eyes.

6   For descriptions of the events labeled Petrus, see John Pemberton, *On the Subject of Java* (Ithaca: Cornell University Press, 1994), pp. 311–318, and Justus M. van der Kroef, " 'Petrus': Patterns of Prophylactic Murder in Indonesia" *Asian Survey* 25, no. 7 (July 1985): 745–759). The political explanation for these killings, that the government wanted to disengage itself from criminals who, having lost their governmental ties, went back to crime and caused disruption, goes only so far. It does not explain, for instance, why the government proceeded illegally, disguising the soldiers who murdered these men nor why they were killed rather than arrested and tried as had been the case from time to time in the past.

7   Soeharto: *Otobiografi: Pikiran, Ucapkan, dan Tindakan Saya [Autobiography: My Thoughts, Speech and Acts],* G. Dwipayana & Ramadhan K. H. (eds.) (Jakarta: PT Citra Lamtoro Gung Persada, 1988), p. 364.

8   The last two sentences in Indonesian are: "Tetapi yang melawan, ya, mau tidak mau harus ditembak. Karena melawan, maka mereka ditembak." The word I translate as resist is melawan, which could also be rendered, "act as an enemy." The sense is that the soldiers came up against an opposed force.

9   Some gangs did use tattoos as signs of their gang membership. But it should be kept in mind that the description of tattoos in *Pos Kota* made no mention of this, instead reporting instances of names of the deceased, their girls friends, pictures of naked

women, and so on. Many people with tattoos who had no connection at all with gangs turned themselves into the police for their own protection. After Petrus had continued for several months, *Tempo* published a short piece on tattoos, showing pictures of men with the tattoos of certain gangs and noting also that, "Of course not all tattoos were of that type. Indeed 15 tattooed men who felt innocent turned themselves in to the Bandung police last week and asked for protection" ("Restless Dragons and Cobras," 18 June 1983).

10 Here see the seminal articles of B.R.O'G. Anderson, "Old Society, New State: Indonesia's New Order in Comparative Perspective" *Journal of Asian Studies* 42:3 (May 1983); and Ruth McVey, "The Beamtenstaat in Indonesia," in B.R.O'G. Anderson and Audrey Kahin (eds.) *Interpreting Indonesian Politics: Thirteen Contributions to the Debate* (Ithaca: Cornell Modern Indonesia Project, 1982).

11 See Daniel S. Lev, "Law is as Law Does: Criminal Procedure in Indonesia" Unpublished paper prepared for the conference "Criminality in Southeast Asia," convened by the Social Science Research Council and the IIAS, held in Amsterdam in March 1997.

12 Siegel, *Fetish, Recognition, Revolution,* (Princeton: Princeton University Press, 1997).

13 See the epilogue to Siegel, *Shadow and Sound: The Historical Thought of a Sumatran People* (Chicago: University of Chicago Press, 1979).

14. The most complete collection of accounts is in Robert Cribb (ed.), *The Indonesian Killings of 1965–66* (Clayton: Monash University Centre of Southeast Asian Studies, 1990). It is not at all the fault of the editor that the accounts are, in general, so sketchy. One would expect accounts written in exile or samizdat, but these are notable for their paucity. For an exception see Pipit Rochijat "Am I or am I not PKI," Ben Anderson (trans.), *Indonesia* 40 (October 1985). See also, on this subject, Siegel, "Yoebar Ayoeb," *Indonesia* 62 (October 1996).

15 See Siegel, *Fetish, Recognition, Revolution,* and the associated literature cited there.

16 Henk Schulte Nordholt with Margreet van Till, "Colonial Criminals on Java 1870–1910." Paper prepared for a conference on criminality in Southeast Asia, Amsterdam, March 20–22.

17 This change is the product of a long history of the development of Indonesian as the language of nationalism and revolution. We pick up this development at the present point of its evolution. For its early phase, I refer the reader to my *Fetish, Recognition, Revolution.*

5 Counter-Revolution Today

1 On September 5, *Pos Kota* had a story with the headline, "Criminologist Doubtful the Perpetrator Wanted to Get Hold of a Pistol: A Certain Police Officer Arrested." The criminologist spoke of the evidence of sadism—the cutting off of the penis and fingers. He thought the criminals had to be considered sadists and that this was more important than their desire to have a pistol as their motive for murder. In this same report, a police agent spoke of the nonplaying captain. The piece is written in such a way as to suggest that wanting a pistol having been eliminated as a motive, the criminals were both sadistic and, at the same time, that a third party was involved. *Pos Kota* did not follow this with further speculation. Instead, in another interview one of those arrested insists on the simple desire for a pistol and the police confirm his opinion. It makes sense to them not as a perversion but as the reasonable demand of a criminal. The

police point out that these people frequented discotheques, smoked ganja, and vandalized their university. They think they know what they wanted the pistol for:

"They admitted that the pistol was for getting money, among other things for menacing those they collected debts from and it is even possible it would be used for other criminal purposes such as robbery and plunder."

The police and the witness agree on the motive—it was simply to have a gun. BH tells his interrogators:

"Every time he saw a policeman in the street, IA always eyed him to see if the policeman had a pistol," BH admitted as it was recorded by a functionary, while adding that purportedly he told friends about his desire to own a pistol last month.

IA was always on the lookout for a policeman with a gun. There is nothing incompatible here with sadism. The criminologist makes it seem as though if one wants to castrate policemen, a process he, the criminologist, describes in some detail, it rules out wanting a gun. But most of us, I think, would see no incompatibility. IA stares at guns whenever he has the chance, we are told. He wants the policeman's instrument of power. He may well be planning to use it. But if he also seems fascinated with it, always on the look out for it, if his desire exceeds the fantasies of using the gun for gain, he may also have dreamed of stealing the police agent's other instrument of power. Or so at least *Pos Kota* suggests. All the more so since, though *Pos Kota* presents Serkap Bambang as a model police officer and a dutiful husband and father, they also print the story of his involvement with another woman adding, at the end, that this was before he was married. And they also print the story of the mysterious woman who points him out to his kidnappers without ever saying just what she wanted him for. In short, he is presented not only as a police officer, but as a sexual being. And so *Pos Kota* makes IA's desire for the instrument understandable as a desire for power in both political and sexual terms.

Whatever he wanted it for, it is evident that the pistol for IA was desirable enough to kill for and desirable enough to make him gaze at it where ever it was to be found. The pistol as a tool of power is evident enough. It makes people disappear. Paired with the policeman's penis, it is also a symbol of power. But what exactly is the urge to castrate here? It is, in the first place, the desire to take power away not from a particular policeman but, as *Pos Kota* presents it, from the police themselves, that part of the state charged with maintaining order and given instruments of force to do so. *Pos Kota*, implicating IA's step father, the supreme court judge, magnifies the danger to the state. It is a desire that arises, in this case, from within the confines of the state. It is more than the desire of a spoiled son for his father's privileges.

2   It may even be that it is for that reason that his own picture does not appear in *Pos Kota* though those of his two accomplices do. But this may have been fear of censorship, pressure on the part of the editors, perhaps even lack of opportunity to obtain his photograph.

3   The reader will note the distance we have come from our first, Lacanian-derived formulation that for lack of a critical word others find a place that contain merely a force of expression without achieving a reference. Here we see the origin of these substitutive words.

4   For an excellent presentation of the role of foreign words in political relations, see Vincente Rafael, *Contracting Colonialism: Transition and Christian Conversion in Taqalog Society Under Early Spanish Rule* (Durham: Duke University Press, 1993). Anderson's remarks are in "The Language of the Indonesian Revolution," *Indonesia* 1 (1996).

James T. Siegel is Professor of Anthropology and Asian
Studies at Cornell University. He is the author of numerous
books including *Fetish, Recognition, Revolution* and *Solo in the
New Order: Language and Hierarchy in an Indonesian City.*

Library of Congress Cataloging-in-Publication Data
Siegel, James T.
A new criminal type in Jakarta : Counter-Revolution today /
James T. Siegel.
ISBN 0-8223-2212-9 (alk. paper).
ISBN 0-8223-2241-2 (pbk. : alk. paper)
1. Political corruption—Indonesia.   2. Misconduct in office—
Indonesia.   3. Political crimes and offenses—Indonesia.
4. Indonesia—Politics and government—1966.
JQ768.5.c6s54   1998   364.1′31′09898—dc21   97-49359 CIP